*Biology and the history of the future*

AN IUBS/UNESCO SYMPOSIUM
with John Cage, Carl-Goeran Heden,
Margaret Mead, John Papaioannou, John Platt,
Ruth Sager, and Gunther Stent

presented by C. H. Waddington, FRS
and published by
Edinburgh University Press

© 1972
International Union of Biological Sciences.
EDINBURGH UNIVERSITY PRESS
22 George Square, Edinburgh
ISBN 0 85224 225 5
*North America*
Aldine — Atherton, Inc.
529 South Wabash Avenue, Chicago
Library of Congress
Catalog Card Number 72-77765
Printed in Great Britain by
T & A Constable, Ltd, Edinburgh

*Biology and the history of the future*

Steve

Science Studies Unit
University of Edinburgh

## Preface

This book is based on a small symposium, organized by myself on behalf of the International Union of Biological Sciences, with further financial help from UNESCO in 1969.

It was, I think, the first that has ever been called together by one of the major international scientific organizations to discuss the relevance of their branch of science to the well-being of mankind in the near future; at any rate, when that is interpreted as something more subtle and rich than can be adequately discussed in terms of providing so many extra tons of carbohydrate or protein, so many extra megawatts of energy. I organized the meeting from the point of view that Biology, the Cinderella of the natural sciences, should now begin to take over from her elder sister Physics in providing the basic philosophical framework within which man forms a picture of his own nature and of the character of those parts of the external world which are most important to him as he tries to realize his own inherent potentials.

The meeting did not attempt to make a complete survey of the potentialities of biology in the near future, or to describe all the 'technological fixes' one might suggest in relation to various problems. There are many other more complete works of this kind, for example, Rattray Taylor's *The Biological Time Bomb* or Nigel Calder's *The Environment Game*, or his *Technopolis*. Our intention was rather to remind ourselves of a few of these possibilities, particularly the less hackneyed ones, and then to relate these to the deeper and less discussed question: what sort of people, living in what sort of societies, do we want to see using these technologies? If we have to 'fix' something, just what is it we have to fix? Our discussions, therefore, and the book which has resulted, continually move backwards and forwards between technological, more or less 'hard' science, and the 'softer' but ultimately perhaps more important fields of psychology and social value. Some readers will probably find this disconcerting, but one of the central convictions underlying the organization of the meeting is that only those who feel at home in both areas will be able to influence the future for the better.

The circumstances that many of the participants were to be at a meeting of the American Association for the Advancement of Science at Dallas, Texas, led us to organize the meeting in a nearby 'average-world' territory, at Chichen Itza, Yucatan, Mexico – not very 'committed' to any of the competing ideologies, and economically midway between the 'undeveloped' and 'fully developed' countries. Unfortunately, the participants from developing countries who had been expected were not in the event able to take part; a Mexican architect-planner and a Chinese-American theoretical biologist found that they could not make it, and Dr M. T. Ragab from Egypt found himself in visa difficulties on arrival, and the Mexican authorities insisted that he return home after only one day.

The accounts of the discussions during the first three days are based on notes kept by John Platt, with a few additions by other people; those for the last two days are edited versions of tape recordings. I have been responsible for editing and rewriting these materials, and the participants should not be held responsible in detail for the words attributed to them.

C. H. WADDINGTON

# Contents

The place of biology                                         1
Personal statements                                          4

TECHNOLOGICAL PROBLEMS
Settlements                                                  7
Wastes and pollution                                         12
Food and applied microbiology                                13
Applied biology – fundamental biology                        22

TOWARDS A POST-INDUSTRIAL WORLD
The situation and our understanding, values, and action      27
The end of Faustian man and the limits of progress           36
Biology and education for the future                         51

Notes                                                        67
Index                                                        70

# The Place of Biology

Up to the present, biology has been the poor sister of the Natural Sciences, over-shadowed by physics and chemistry with their technological offspring in engineering and manufacturing industry. It is often said today that the First Technological Age is nearly over, and that man is passing into a new phase of civilization which will be based on something other than the simple physical sciences. The candidate usually put forward to take over the dominant role is described sometimes as Automation or, in a more general sense, as Communication Science. There is, however, a case for arguing that the fact of Automation or Communication is less important than what the systems are automated to do or to communicate, and that the science which will contribute the content, even if not the tools, of the new civilization will, and perhaps should, be biology.

This case has two main facets: *technological*, which argues that the most challenging unsolved technical problems of the near future are basically biological — food, population increase, deterioration of the environment; and *philosophical*, which suggests that the modes of thought, the concepts and the type of understanding sought for in biology would give a bio-technical' world a set of values and an emotional tone radically different from those of the physio-technical world of today (whether Capitalist or Socialist), and much more favourable for the solution of the grave social and psychological problems which mankind faces.

## Bio-technologies : Challenges, Promises, and Threats

For the greater part of the world — the 'developing' part — the near future presents, with terrifying urgency, two major challenges: population control and food production. The former appears to be wholly within the biological-social field, to be solved by some advance — perhaps the long-awaited aphrodisiac contraceptive — to which new physical knowledge is unlikely to make any contribution. Food is, again, a product of biology. Its production can be increased by pumping in more power, tractors, fertilizers, and so on; but the physical technology of these factors is already well understood. The technical challenges are much more in such biological fields as the avoidance of environmental pollution by the run-off of fertilizers, herbicides, or pesticides, or the exploitation of new sources of protein (leaf protein, bacterial or algal growth on otherwise unusable substrates, and so on). Even if we have to rely on artificial synthesis of amino-acids, fats, carbohydrates, and so on, the greater part of the technology seems likely to depend on reproducing biological processes such as photosynthesis, cell-free ribosome systems, and so on.

There is considerable public interest and anxiety in some of the promises and challenges offered by advances in biomedical science, such as organ transplantation. The possibilities of manipulations of the reproductive processes (long-term storage of sperm, ova transplantation, sex determination, nuclear transplantation, and so on) may soon become even more challenging.

In the improvement of the environment for human living, many of the major problems of the near future have a strong if not predominant biological component, since they demand an increased capacity to control the natural processes within the biosphere. Examples are supplies of fresh pure water, cleansing the atmosphere, preservation and rehabilitation of the countryside and natural vegetation.

An allied problem is the guidance of the process of urbanization, which is proceeding at an almost explosive rate, into directions in which the new urban areas provide greater satisfaction of human physiological needs than they have done in the recent past. We are still scandalously ignorant of exactly what are the conditions (of noise, polluted air, accelerations and decelerations, lack of muscular exercise, stressful stimuli, and so on) under which 'normal' life is carried on by various categories of citizens (commuters, office workers, salesmen, industrial workers, labourers, and so on); and we have little information about the biologically optimum conditions which ought to be aimed at.

*The Relevance of Biological Types of Thought*

This century has seen a series of massive revolts against the previously accepted values of Western civilization. The Marxist revolt was followed by the Colonial revolt; and now young people are involved, on a world-wide scale which encompasses East, West, and the Developing Countries, in a so-far unco-ordinated set of movements, typified by the Beats, Hippies, Flower People, Castroists, Guevarists, Maoists, and the widespread Student Movements. Most of the recent movements are occurring in a sphere which is much broader and deeper than mere politics and economics; they are concerned with the total character of human life and its social setting. Many of the movements express an outspoken antagonism, not only to existing technology, but to rational and logical thought as a whole; but since the movements have found most of their adherents among the sections of society which are illiterate in logic and technics, it is not easy to assess just what their statements really imply. Certainly few of the protesters give any sign of being ready to escape from man's most complex technological achievement — the city — and return to the hard manual agricultural labour which was the common lot before the advent of the competitive-technological system which they so much — and so justifiably — dislike.

The kinds of rationality and of technology from which much of modern youth seeks to disassociate itself have been moulded in the main by the need to understand the physical non-living world and the desire to exploit its potentials. It has been usual to accept physics as the paragon among the sciences, and to take, as the exemplar of what rational thought should be, most usually the already outmoded 'classical' fully deterministic logic of Newtonian physics, occasionally rendered slightly more subtle by an admixture of the indeterminacy of quantum theory, which mollifies the old rigidity only by stochastic, and not at all by any humanizing, component. On the technological level, the appropriate attitude has been to maximize some variable in a few-component system — get more power-output per unit of fuel per kilogramme of engine per cost of fabrication, and let anything else go hang. Now these attitudes not only seem totally foreign and obnoxious to the Beat-Hippie crowd of conceptual illiterates, but they seem shallow and pretty boring to most intellectually sophisticated biologists.

Students of living things, who approach them on their own terms, have to develop types of thinking capable of dealing with entities of extreme complexity which yet exhibit global characters of a definite — and therefore in some sense simple — kind. In the biological world almost nothing is maximized — except some variable, which no one has yet satisfactorily defined, important for evolution, and related not to the organism under immediate consideration, but to the number of its offspring — and even that is maximized only over the long term of many generations, not just from one generation to the next. And, most importantly, there are in biology no timeless, eternal, or universal laws, like those of physics; every biological unit has a history, indeed one might say, *is* a history — a circumstance which physicists who come into biology tend at first to find unnerving (cf. Delbruck, *A Physicist Looks at Biology*). In place of the maximization of entities whose essence is independent of time, biology deals in the main with optimization, or balancing, or 'Golden-Rule-izing', of things which are very complex, and which have histories, and whose stability and balance are going to be tested over a long period — a number of generations. The kind of understanding it attempts to achieve, of its most general subject matters (such as evolution), is much more akin to the kind of understanding of human history we aim at, than that which physics gives us of the interactions of any nameless oxygen atom with a couple of nameless hydrogen atoms. Biologists do not attempt to say of living things in general (it

3

may be different of a few matters of detail) that so-and-so *must* happen, but rather this seems to have happened, and after all it's quite easy to see how it might have done so.

Another characteristic of biology is the thorough-going way in which it transcends the physicist's simple-minded distinction between the subject and the object. An evolving population, by the behaviour of its members, chooses – or creates – the environment which exerts natural selective pressures on it. There is no pre-ordained rat-race; the biologist is studying situations in which the possibility of 'dropping-out' – migrating elsewhere – is always available. Again, biologists who study perception, or the acquisition of knowledge and understanding of the external world by the developing child, find themselves forced to recognize that in neither of these processes is the subject merely a passive recipient of whatever the 'objective' imposes on it. On the contrary, both in learning how the world works, and even in apprehending it in perception, an active and indeed creative participation of the 'subject' is essential (cf., for example, Piaget, *Biology and Knowledge*; Gregory, *Eye and Brain*). A drop-out who objects to being treated as a 'thing' would have to think again if he was in a world dominated by a biologically-oriented outlook which denied that there are any 'things' quite independent of the subjects who observe them.

## Personal Statements

WADDINGTON. There are four themes to consider:

1. application of biology to world-human problems, especially the well-known biology;
2. same for 'far-out' biology;
3. centrality of biology in education; and
4. the relation of biology to development of Systems-of-Value which are appropriate or congruent to the way mankind is going to evolve.

The central theme of biology is the problem of optimizing the components of a system so as to maximize the whole, rather than maximizing any single component.

'We live in a "people-killing culture" ... We need conditions in which the *primacy of the person* can be realised ... (Our Society) *grinds up* human beings.' [Wasteland culture, in *Anarchy* 88 (1967)].

It is important to remember, with all our changes, and those ahead, that *society has to keep operating* ... We can't afford to have a 'hippie' casualness about our water supply! I suggest that each of us should start off by making a personal statement on his own concern in these areas.

4

MEAD. A relation between *biological individuality and the nature of knowledge* is needed ... Men once (in some countries) knew why men were born, and died, and so on ... either through practical knowledge or through the actions of supernaturals, but they had a world-picture, a framework. ... We need to be aware of the whole. We need models (of the world) that include not only what we do know, but boxes for what we don't know.

STENT. My interest is in *the decay of motivation.*

HEDEN. We must discuss *professional ethics* in the application of biology ... We need trans-disciplinary relations — people who are willing to talk about things *outside* their speciality ... We need them to approach the most important issues: *Biology and Human Rights.*

PLATT. My interests lie in the *Intellectual Urgencies* of the next ten years (There are two major crises ahead, nuclear war and famine). And in the need to have a 'humanized image of the twenty-first century' to guide and inspire.

CAGE. We need a plan that *leaves us free to do what we are capable of doing.* We are coming into an age of abundance; for example, in music, there is not just one single strain of development. *Wanting* is one of the things that may disappear ... I am reading Thoreau as a possible guide ... Crises are good for people — every crisis in New York *brings people together*! Also, *we need to get the environment to work.*

SAGER. I started in politics, and then abandoned it for science. Now, with the present spirit of rebellion, I am optimistic — I wish I was 20 years old again!

*We need a positive kind of value system.* The idea of 'the new rights of man' encompasses the opportunity to be oneself, to live in a world that has a kind of human dignity. The purpose of this conference is 'to use biology (its principles, and examples; and reasoning and applications) to save the world', in just the same way that Buckminster Fuller's purpose is 'to use architecture (and principles of design) to save the world'. But Fuller's has been written up and organized while Wad's idea has not — and could be. We need Ideology and Organization; and maybe a book on *change* to teach people a right picture of the world.

I don't know what is relevant to tell my students, that is *meaningful* about where they can go.

PAPAIOANNOU. I am concerned with the structure of human settlements ... the biological aspects of human needs.

*The next thirty years is going to be a continuous crisis.* Only around the turn of the century (2000) will there be some let-up, some return to stabilities and satisfactions.

## Technological Problems

Settlements
Wastes and Pollution
Food and Applied Microbiology
Applied Biology – Fundamental Biology

# Settlements

PAPAIOANNOU. Most people seem to agree on figures for the population of the world which are not very far from 7 billion by the year 2000. This figure is not difficult to assess. After that date forecasting difficulties increase, but I should say that in 100 years we shall arrive near the figure of 20 billion. The curve of population growth must essentially have an S-shape, and eventually the rate of increase must level off. It is very difficult to forecast when this will begin to happen. It is in fact one of the major issues of social policy for World Man. But there must certainly be an intermediate period of extremely rapid growth

In addition to these estimates of configurations in space and numbers of population, our group in Athens has made some calculations about income, which we have checked with a great number of economists in different parts of the world. In 100 years from now income will have reached a high level, with no illiteracy and the elimination of many things we find terrible today. There will be a great degree of affluence by that time. That does not, of course, mean that people will be happy — maybe they will feel they require much more.

One thing which is interesting is that the gap between the rich and poor countries, according to these projections, *increases* — without any hope of decreasing — to a bit beyond the year 2000. This is a major point. After that, if we get through it, the gap will start decreasing steadily until it is reduced to about one third or one quarter of what it is today. This means a considerable levelling off of the differences between rich and poor countries, so much so that the tensions will become smaller. But during the next thirty or forty years we have these tensions increasing.

In the same period we have also the problem of food. In 100 years from now there will probably be enough food for all, but today we do have a serious problem of food, and the majority of specialists think that this is one of the major crises which humanity will be facing in the next twenty years. We had experts who calculated that several hundred million, or even one billion, people may die from malnutrition between now and the year 2000. Of course there is a fraction of experts, I would say about one quarter, who believe that we can overcome this, basing their view, for instance, on the success of dwarf wheat here in Mexico, in India, and in Pakistan, which has been one of the most spectacular successes, and on the rice produced in the International Rice

7

Institute in the Philippines. They take this as a sign that the adaptation can take place much more quickly and that we can overcome the crisis.

But there is another aspect to the crisis. My first point was ' income gap, the second was the food gap; the third is the settlement crisis. It has been estimated that between now and the year 2000 the amount of building that is going to take place is between two and three times what humanity has invested in building from its beginning up to the year 1960. Thus, there is a major crisis in human settlements ahead of us for the next 30 years or so. This is perhaps the only major discontinuity in the evolution of settlements by size that we have had in human history.

If we take the larger settlements of the past, they were all of about one million people − Constantinople, Chang-An, Rome, Angkor Wat, and others. That was about the maximum in mediaeval history. This size was reached again about 1800 in cities like London and Tokyo. Then, in about 150 years, the maximum rose from about one million to about ten million − London, Tokyo, and New York. So up to the beginning of this century we had about a tenfold increase in about five generations. We expect now, within not five generations but one, from now to the year 2000, to have another leap by a factor of ten, that is, to reach the 100-million urban unit. But the leap is not only in population but also in area. The area of urban units will increase not tenfold but more like 100-fold, and the internal complexity by a probably still higher factor. This is the leap from the metropolis to megalopolis, which is a complex of cities usually in some kind of linear arrangement, which are strongly interrelated in a way that influences the whole space between these cities.

WADDINGTON. Although these agglomerations will in some sense be single-functional units, I suppose most of the people in them will also feel that they belong to smaller groupings or neighbourhoods, as Londoners today may belong to Chelsea or Hampstead and New Yorkers to Manhattan or the Bronx.

PAPAIOANNOU. At the moment we are a little at a loss how to approach the question of smaller units, because we are at a turning point where the urban community in the old sense is being destroyed or lost and disintegrated. There are certain signs that we are in a transition period, which will hopefully help to revive the small scale community in the way which is necessary in the near future. This disintegration has been much more pronounced in the more developed countries, and the urban spirit is still much more alive in countries at a lower level of development. For instance, in Greece it seems to be still alive. In the 'Human Community' project which we are doing for Athens,† we found it there quite consistently, with local life organized around particular lively nuclei. Communities like that appear quickly as a city is developing.

Towards the outskirts, you find a number of people getting together at low densities with some rudimentary shopping centre forming in the middle of the area. This gets reinforced, and you get progressively higher level functions concentrating at this point. When the people come sufficiently close together they feel they belong to one community and they give it a name It is quite conscious for all of them and they develop a kind of community life around that little nucleus.

This community evolves according to a certain pattern, which has been more or less constant in Athens for the last two or three generations. That is, they grow from very low densities to higher densities with an increasing feeling of togetherness. At the beginning things are very dynamic, they change quickly, but in the end, when this community becomes incorporated in the main part of the city, developments are slower and become static, and in a way the community disintegrates again towards the end of its life. This is a temporal cycle, taking from beginning to end a period of 30, 40, or 50 years, but the process has also a spatial expression at any given moment. If you take a radial section of the city from periphery to centre, you find communities which are consecutively at all these stages of evolution. In the case of a country of average economic development like Greece, the stages are quite real and quite well developed. We intend to embark on the study of similar units in other countries, but this we haven't yet been able to do in a sufficiently advanced way. We only know that in places like the United States this scheme does not apply in the same way. The units there are considerably larger.

PLATT. I should like to mention one aspect of this – the overlapping governmental units involved in big complexes of this sort. Richard Meier has made a study of this. He finds there are some 465 semi-independent governmental organizations in the San Francisco Bay area for a population of about four million people. Roughly one governmental unit per 10,000; although, of course, some of them actually cover the whole area. This includes school districts, garbage units, councils of various sorts, economic units. The problem is to get these semi-independent government bodies interrelated so that initiating any new project does not require an almost infinite number of signatures, or so that one of these bodies isn't doing something that another one is negating. This is a fantastic problem already at the four-million level; to extend this to the 100-million level is going to require new levels of organization and management

WADDINGTON. At this ratio of governing bodies to people a megalopolis of 100-million would be run by something like 10,000 different agencies. The possibility of an administrative jam-up occurring, so that some essential service just doesn't operate, would be enormous.

PLATT. The complexity probably goes up as the square of the number of units of units of organization or management.

WADDINGTON. Is anybody seriously studying this as a problem in organizing a management structure? How far do our universities deal with this? Presumably the legal profession, the management profession, and people of this kind have got to work out how it is to be done. This is going to happen within one generation. There is not much time.

PLATT. Many people are aware that there is a problem because of their own difficulties of getting things done; but the number who are aware of the total managerial complexity, and who are trying to do something scientific about it, is very small.

HEDEN. And we need to extrapolate this growth further till we come to Ecumenopolis?

PAPAIOANNOU. Yes. After a time the megalopolitan areas will start overlapping or merging into each other. Little by little they will start forming networks of megalopolises, which will be still higher and larger units and eventually this will lead to the Ecumenopolis, and interconnected stable urban network over the whole world.

PLATT. My feeling is that if we can solve the problem of the transition to the megalopolis, the hundred-million unit, the further transition to the five-billion will be much easier.

PAPAIOANNOU. Yes, exactly. This step that we are now facing is the most difficult one. This is why I mentioned this as well as food and population as the third of the major problems mankind will have to face between now and the year 2000. These are tremendous challenges. Humanity may very easily fail in one of these and if it fails in any one of them it is lost. Of course the first answer of many people is to say 'Why have Ecumenopolis?, why not abolish it?' but I would say that this is impossible.† I would say that this movement is a *chreod*; that is, that the evolution from metropolis towards megalopolis seems to be almost inevitable. People like living in big cities, for many reasons. Megalopolis does offer many more advantages of all kinds. We know that people today are tending to move toward these great megalopolitan regions. It is something that is going to happen, at least for the next few decades, and our problem is not to destroy them but to make them work.

MEAD. People tend to move into the cities now because in most cases you starve less in the cities than you do in the country. This does not need to continue. This trend towards megalopolis, that we keep on saying is *the* trend, is based on archaic methods of building, archaic methods of transportation, and the non-application of almost every new technique we know. To extrapolate from an archaic period, has, I think, its dangers. It ought to be recognized that this is not inevitable unless we make it so. We are not dealing with something like

10

the population explosion, which we know we can't stop within a certain amount of time. There are many, many devices which could be used to stop this if we didn't like this design.

PAPAIOANNOU. Instead of saying 'stopping', I would say to control it.

MEAD. Control it, divert it, differentiate it. To the extent that this gets stated as an inevitable process following from some inexorable law, this will make it come true.

PLATT. But distinguish here, Margaret, between the things that are inexorable and the things that can be changed. The things that are inevitable in the next twenty or thirty years include much of this growth of population and much of this growth of megalopolis. Saying it is not inexorable will mean that you neglect it.

MEAD. No, I don't agree that it is inexorable. If the amount of new planning and new research and new control that will be necessary to run these places were used in other ways to spread the population more evenly over the surface of large countries, to centres of attraction of low order, they could give every single thing that megalopolis gives.

PAPAIOANNOU. How then do you explain that all over the developed world at the present time, in Japan, in the United States, in England, or in Central Europe, this process is going on?

MEAD. Of course, it has happened, but it has happened just at the height of industrialization, not in the coming post-industrial state where we really use the techniques that we possess. None of these cities is founded on the techniques that we now have. Look at New York, it is absolutely archaic in every possible way.

WADDINGTON. Maybe one could, in theory, stop the drive towards Ecumenopolis. But it would take time. The movement we see today looks as though it had a pretty large momentum which would have to be counteracted before the trend to centralization could be reversed. In any case, is anyone seriously trying to stop it at present? In my opinion we had better get ready to deal with this trend for the next thirty years at least.

PAPAIOANNOU. I want to say something more about the question of whether we should try to abolish large units because they would be inhuman or monstrous. I take the position that it is not the size or the state of the units which matters, it is simply the kind of internal organization that they have. We believe, and we have enough evidence, that you can design megalopolis and even Ecumenopolis in such a way as to be not only human, but so that it can provide all the utilities, all the choices, and all the opportunities, in a much *increased* degree. It could constitute something that will be a real advantage to humanity, provided that you organize it correctly. You have

11

to have the right units at each level. If the world is going to have a population of ten or twenty billion, you will need to have certain authorities that work on a world-wide scale. And with increased spread and increased circulation of people there will need to be many organizations on this scale — but, you will have to control other things at the level of continents, and others at the level of the countries or regions of today, and others at the local level. The local level is something which should not be disregarded It seems that we shall need more devices that make the *home* very important again, and the local community just around the home. Thus we require the entire range of organizations, from the largest scale to the smallest.


## Wastes And Pollution

HEDEN. I think many of the most important problems of the present time arise from the inadequacy of organization at the largest scale. The area of authority of existing authorities is not wide enough. For instance, the Ruhr-Rhine area in Germany is the source of sulphur dioxide which may have profound effects on the total biological productivity in forests and fields in Sweden, where some of the pollutants are deposited by rain. We have this problem *now*, it is not something in the future. We in Sweden can't do much about the industries of Northern Europe using high-sulphur coal.

PLATT. Let me not belittle any of these real concerns about pollution which are important to all of us, but some of these cases are well on the way to being solved. An outcry on pollutants has been raised now for several years, and some companies have begun to respond with better chemicals. I think there is, for instance, no non-biodegradable detergent sold any longer in the United States. The detergent pollution problem has gone down to one-tenth or maybe one-hundredth of what it was. As for DDT, dozens of groups are working on it and they are finding other insecticide methods, including highly specialized insect attractants and the 'sterile male' method to deal with the problem. These are problems which I don't think a group like us has to work on at the moment, because they are already being studied technically and there will be better solutions within a very few years. What no groups are working on are the problems of the social structures which lie ahead, and here it is crucial to get some new approaches started.

HEDEN. I must say that I am very worried about participatory democracy in this connection. I do not think that participatory democracy is good for producing utilities. There is no sense of responsibility for the whole situation; one community

12

shoots its pollution over to the next one. For producing utilities I think one must find other types of system.

PAPAIOANNOU. It is not just a problem of *producing* things as utilities; a major problem in cities is to get rid of the waste products. This is not only waste material; an important waste-product of civilization is waste energy — heat. Atomic energy power plants and desalination plants could be located at special places near the coasts, particularly where the continental shelf is narrow and there is access to deep water.

PLATT. But there is no way of getting around the thermal pollution they create; it is a thermodynamic impossibility to get rid of this heat.

STENT. I don't accept the thermodynamic impossibility. You could use endothermic reactions, and there are things like nuclear condensations which in fact absorb energy.

WADDINGTON. The trouble is that it is *low temperature* heat that you have to get rid of, which makes it more difficult. But biological systems can use low temperature energy, to synthesize more rapidly. Large gains could be obtained from 'waste heat' by biological methods.† In fact they really *must* be obtained if we are to avoid catastrophic famine. Remember the fantastically big returns which are being reaped in India from new varieties of wheat, maize, and rice, developed by very small-scale work on plant breeding for tropical climates. The wheats and maize were produced mainly under the auspices of the Rockefeller Foundation, who financed a small group in Mexico comprising I suppose not more than thirty or forty scientists. These Mexican dwarf varieties of wheat, which essentially cut down on forming stem and put all the energy into producing grain instead — diverting the physiology of the plant a bit — took only a few years to adapt to the Indian circumstances. Think of the number of biologists there are around the world and what an effect a minute fraction of them have had, when put on to a really crucial problem.

PLATT. Yet this is still mainly done by Foundations and Institutes. It always astonishes me that it is not done by private capital, because these enormous returns come in quite short periods. It seems to me that if we could only mobilize the profit motivation more in such cases it could amplify immensely the scale and effectiveness of this kind of urgent Research and Development work.

## Food and applied microbiology

HEDEN. How does one create awareness about the potential impacts which applied biology could have? The problems are certainly challenging enough as indicated by the 'three wishes' which I formulated a year or two ago at a Fermentation

13

Conference. They were the sort of gifts I would ask from a good fairy, if I met one. The *first* was a solid-phase enzyme reactor, small and simple enough to do the job of making a nitrogen fertilizer directly from the air, in any small Indian town. The *second* would be a sewage converter with the methane oxidized and the carbon dioxide photosynthetically bound, that would turn out undenatured protein suitable for spinning meat analogues or for coagulation to make cheese. The *third* would be a starter pill (micro-encapsulated bacteria resistant to a heat labile antibiotic included for contamination control, together with growth factors and minerals), which would be centrally manufactured but could be used in small protein-starved communities to turn a brew of cassava or other cheap starch into a lysine-rich soup. I am a great believer in primitive fermentations as a means to overcome acceptability problems. However, they must be switched from alcohol production, which is the usual aim of these methods, and also the dangers which some of them may involve (such as mycotoxins in mixed and uncontrolled microbial populations) must be eliminated.

Consider the first, *nitrogen fixation*. There the situation is as follows: South America, tropical Africa, and India utilize at present between a tenth and a twentieth as much chemical nitrogen fertilizer per arable acre as is used in countries like Russia, Siberia, and the Eastern European group. To bring the developing countries up even to that rather modest level would cost about three billion dollars per year, and would require an investment of about 4,200 billion dollars. That doesn't consider the fact that there is a tremendous transport problem, and doesn't take into consideration at all the fact that besides nitrogen you must mobilize phosphorous and potassium, and of these we have already used the most easily accessible deposits, so that they are becoming more and more difficult. Against this you can set biological nitrogen fixation. It is well known that an acre of alfalfa which is well nodulated, that is, its roots carry many nodules containing nitrogen-fixing micro-organisms called *Rhizobia*, can add up to about 200 kilograms of nitrogen out of the air to the soil. So here is the way to improve the nitrogen fertilizing situation, by using the bacteria as small microscopic factories. It is obvious then that this is very important and should be the subject of a major effort, but how many groups of scientists do you think are doing genetics on *Rhizobia*? To my knowledge — and I looked into this a bit — there are *four* groups, making a total of about ten people in the world. Because all the micro-biologists — I talk with all respect for the molecular biologists who have contributed so fantastically much to biology — will all work on *E. coli* K12 or *E. coli* B. There seems to be no force on earth that can put some of them on to *Rhizobia* or other areas of direct practical significance.

STENT. The *E. coli* molecular genetics is coming to an end . . . I think this might be something to take over from it. You want to get the idea going in the leading graduate schools like Harvard, MIT, Berkeley, and such places. I think this might have tremendous effect. It is precisely the sort of thing a lot of people are looking for. They are tired of larking around and following one more academic point with another. Whether it is one sub-unit or two sub-units — nobody actually cares any more. What they want to do is something significant. What Heden is saying is what I think they would consider significant. All this army of graduates who are just coming out, they are anxious for this kind of thing.

PLATT. They are begging for it. But there is still a sociological barrier. The history of academic biology has been the history of the individual worker, and that, of course, is not applied work; and the academic work has been disconnected from the agricultural experimental stations. I think in the next five years one of the great developments will be the appearance of biological *Route 128s*† round the major universities — little companies to exploit one or another of these developments. It would be healthy.

This is a good example of what I see as the absolute emergency.† We have got to treat this problem of the world as we would a war. Just in the same way as we mobilized the very best scientists in the country to fight submarines or to develop atomic energy or radar, we have got to get the very best people in biology working on problems of this sort, in an applied way. We have got to do it, as a kind of sacrifice, I think, for 10 or 20 years — long enough to get us past this crucial time — then they can go back, or their students can go back.

HEDEN. I think microbiologists should be reminded of the effects which vaccination, antibiotics, the control of epidemics, and so on, have had on the population increase. You should put this to them, and then explain what can be done on the other side of the balance. I have mentioned nitrogen fixation and photosynthesis — but take areas like veterinary vaccines, and there is an important form of biological control, which is essentially using viruses and bacteria for controlling insects and pests. This is a field which I think is particularly interesting, because it could automatically suck up very much of the capability and technology which has been developed by the Biological Warfare people.

I should like to bring out a few additional areas in the field I know about. One thing that is particularly dear to my heart is the potential of microbiology in foreign aid, in helping developing countries. I think this has been badly underestimated. One has forgotten that those economies export raw materials like sugar and starch, just the sort of materials with which many microbiologists work. This is an area where one should put in a lot of effort. There has, for instance, been conspicuous success in growing sugar cane cells in fermentors on a very cheap starch material, which they can break down to sugar. The industrial use may be quite far in the future, but it's a worrying prospect that the highly industrialized societies may start to produce even more of the sucrose they need than they do at the present time. Then we would have a situation similar to what we have had in rubber and fibres — taking away from the developing countries one of their few exports. Instead we should try to see what new uses we can give them for their starch, sugar, and so on.

There are actually a fantastic number of methods to upgrade those materials. For instance, one could use them as a basis for microbial cultures producing edible protein, and this is certainly an important area. I think it might be even more important to make use of the potential of microbial enzymes, and to bring into the developing countries techniques which are so sophisticated that they have not really yet got started even in the developed countries. Take solid-state enzymology; you tie the enzyme to some solid matrix, and then you do the enzyme reaction, in a glass column for instance.† This we know can be done, it is a relatively new technique, and it has the great advantage that it does away with having very heavy catalytic reactors operating at 200 atmospheres and 700°C, or something like that. Now if you have those reactors already, as the chemical industry in the United States and Europe has, then you might do research in solid state enzymology because you want to be in the forefront of it, but you do it just so that you are prepared, and you hope to God that it won't develop into a major undertaking elsewhere, because you have so much investment in heavy stuff. However, a developing country could, as it were, cut down underneath into a completely new type of chemical industry. If you combine solid state enzymology with industrial gel filtration, for instance, which is now coming up fast, and many of the gels are in fact microbial products — you could start something quite new in a country like Cuba, where there is a lot of sugar. This is, of course, a fantastically expensive and difficult project to get started, and I can't visualize that it will be done by anything less than a major international body. At the present time, what is done in this area is done by big industrial companies, which are not necessarily progressive. Most of the important single-cell protein research is done by a handful of very big oil companies. They have two interests. One is of course to improve the quality of the oil by deparaffinization; the other is to make protein. I have an uneasy feeling that they regard this as a bit of a gimmick for getting new concessions — now I am perhaps too cynical but it is probably why they have been so active.

WADDINGTON. Is this beyond the small firm? This is the kind of thing that the *Route 128* industries around Boston did in

16

electronics. Could young bright chaps setting up little firms on their own do it, or does it need really massive resources?

PLATT. I reckon that in biology a little firm would need, for the initial steps in such projects, of the order of five senior scientists for about three years at a minimum — say 200,000 dollars.

HEDEN. In the biochemical industry one has a rule of thumb — I don't know quite how true it is — that a completely new product costs about 5 million dollars.

PLATT I think if you start in existing buildings you can start with money of the order of $200,000 a year. Of course, if you have to put up buildings for the research group, that requires capital of about another 3—5 million. Let me emphasize, however, that the payback in many of these biological operations could be from 3—50 times what it is in the electronic industry. It is fantastic. I think there could be many billion-dollar pay-offs from million-dollar investments in biological projects in the next few years.

HEDEN. Well, there is a very nice example, since we are talking about developing countries, in the Syntex Company in Mexico. They use a natural resource to make cortisone, and as the next step they developed progesterone. Birth control steroids actually came out of a research project started here in Mexico.

PLATT. Another self-maintaining group, more like the *Route 128* type, is the Wisconsin Alumni Research Foundation, WARF. Their first big patent was for enriching vitamin B in milk by irradiation. This gave them enough millions to support additional research. Their next big pay-off was Warfarin — that is, dicoumarol used for poisoning of rats — the biggest rat-killer in the world, and now that is bringing in even more. I believe a big fraction of the research support of the University of Wisconsin now comes from this WARF operation. What we need is fifty other biological R & D firms or foundations like that.

HEDEN. If one takes the needs of the developing countries really seriously then it might be a good idea to develop a meat analogue. This is something which could be done quite quickly. The technique for spinning protein fibres is well established, but the practical application of raw materials to make meat analogue is limited to a few. In many areas there is sugar in plenty; for instance, in Ethiopia, they have a big sugar factory which produces some 30,000 tons of molasses per year, but most of it is used to bind dust on the roads, because no better use has been found for it. So there is a lot of raw material for making yeast. You can also use oil to make microbial protein, and also natural gas, and there is plenty of that in various parts of the world. Using each of these raw materials constitutes a research project in itself. They all have a common denominator, but not much effort has been put into studying it. That is large-scale transformation of the protein into a meat analogue. We know that it can be done with soya protein. You spin the soya protein in a bath, so that you get fine fibres, and you provide those fibres with a bit of taste by adding appropriate amino acids and extracts. What comes out is something called meat analogue and not meat substitute, because in many ways it's better than meat. This can be done with soya protein which is easy to coagulate; if you want to do the same thing with microbial protein you must get it out of the cell. But the cell wall of a bacterium is not easy to break up, so techniques to get the protein out without denaturization must be developed. If you denature it you cannot manipulate it — you can't make cheese or meat analogues or anything like that. I am confident that this can be solved. In my own lab we have worked out disintegration techniques which cost about 3 cents per kilogram, which begins to be a reasonable cost, but one should try to get a further reduction, perhaps down to about one-fifth of that.

When it comes to improving the situation for developing countries one has to take into consideration that even if you can make a lot of protein in the form of a yellow powder in a plastic bag, people won't eat it, because they aren't used to it. You must take their basic psychological needs into account. In very many developing countries there are traditional fermentation techniques, producing primitive beers and such things. They often have the advantage that they improve the shelf life of perishable products, and they may even improve them a bit from the nutritional point of view, but all of them are based on a randomly mixed microbial population which happens to be around. I see no reason why we could not provide those people, who have this sort of fermentation experience, with 'starters' in the form of pills, which could be made cheaply on a large scale. You would have to make use of novel techniques like encapsulation; you provide coatings for the bacteria so that they stand up very long in a dry state, and you would also encapsulate critical nutrients which one might have to add. If you want to turn cassava — which is an abundant starchy material — into a broth or soup, rich in nutritionally valuable substances, you would probably have to include some biotin and probably some salts in the pill. It is also quite possible that you would include an antibiotic which would control the contaminants so that a sterile fermentation technique would not be necessary. Of course, your starter micro-organisms would have to be resistant to the drug used. I think that a new antibiotic would be desirable, because you wouldn't like to accelerate the appearance of resistance against antibiotics used for treating people who are sick; and the antibiotic should be destroyed upon heating so that when the material is cooked the antibiotic is inactivated. The important thing is that you would, so to speak, have to lower yourself to non-industrial preparation, so that you would give people a feeling that they were making the product themselves. I think this is the only quick way to achieve acceptance. They would know that it was just their traditional product in a slightly improved form.

Referring to nitrogen fixation, I think that if you put enough man-power on to it – maybe 1/100th or 1/1000th of what you put into a space project – perhaps a couple of hundred people, it should be possible to develop biological nitrogen fixation to the point where you could actually make use of the enzyme process itself, in a solid phase system. You would have a column where you move air in at one end and get a nitrogen fertilizer out at the other. This may sound very difficult to do but I don't think it is that hard, and it would be exceedingly important, because even though the size of the nitrogen fertilizer factories have been reduced continuously in the last few decades, they are still very major operations if they are going to turn out a cheap product. It means that in India you would need maybe a dozen giant factories, and then you have enormous transport problems.

WADDINGTON. And heat pollution problems.

HEDEN. Yes, well, that also; you must have a lot of energy, of course, so an enzymatic process would be much better, because it would solve your transport problems and economize on energy.

MEAD. (to Heden) What was next on your list of gifts from the good fairy?

HEDEN. Well, this is a fantastically fortuitous list. Let's take the next one as being concerned with recirculation of sewage. It would be a unit that takes sewage and turns out clean water, a fertilizer, and a nutritious meat analogue. Here I think it is also important to realize the importance of microbiology. We can, in principle, turn most biological materials over into methane, carbon dioxide, and hydrogen, and those com-pounds can all be transformed into microbial protein. Methane conversion is probably the most generally known. In most sewage plants you produce a lot of this gas, and in principle it is easy to clean it up and pipe it to another installation for conversion into a protein. This is, I think, still not an economic proposition, because of the fact that the process needs so much air. However, I wouldn't be astonished if it is found possible to do it economically if you incorporate a step involving chemical catalysis.

The second gas is hydrogen. You can get hydrogen out of a recirculatory sewage system, but another possibility is using hydrogen from electrolysis. If we produce very much elec-tricity by nuclear reactors we will certainly have the pos-sibility of producing cheap hydrogen. Schlegel in Germany has found *Hydrogenomonas* bacteria which are extremely efficient in turning this over into protein; you get 33 grams of protein per kilowatt hour. You use a medium which contains no chloride, and then you put your electrodes right into the fermentor, providing the cells with both the oxygen and the hydrogen which they need, so it's a very simple system. This is one of the protein sources which I think might become important, because hydrogen is a relatively common thing.

The third gas, carbon dioxide, is something which one must consider from the point of view that there will certainly still be a lot of things which we will burn. Of course, one can use the carbon dioxide to increase the productivity of plants, in hot houses, but one can also use it for making different kinds of algal protein. Of these the most promising at the present time is *Spirulina platensis*. This is a spiral-shaped micro-organism, which was isolated some five or six years ago and which the Institut Francais du Petrol has done a great deal of work on. Its great advantage is that it grows at a very alkaline pH, and this means that it keeps clean, since there is nothing else much that can grow in the environment. Also, when you add carbon dioxide to such an alkaline medium it is economically used — it doesn't bubble through, but just goes into solution immediately. Finally, the organisms are spiral-shaped — it's a beautiful micro-organism designed just for this purpose! When it photosynthesizes, it creates small oxygen bubbles and those seem to be caught inside the spirals, so the cells float to the surface, and there the density gets so high that they screw into each other, so that you get long fibres. This means that you don't have to use centrifuges or anything like that for harvesting. You can just strain them off. It has a very high productivity which compares favourably with *Chlorella*. Also it has good protein quality, not too different from casein. The Institut Francais du Petrol has been playing with the idea of building a factory in the Sahara which would produce 10,000 tons per year. There natural gas would be burnt to make carbon dioxide and, of course, there is plenty of sunlight.

PLATT. Has the economics of this production actually been worked out? Remember great hopes were held for algal photosynthesis a few years ago, but when it came down to preparing the plastics or concrete tanks, by the time you'd paid for the capital investment and washing and cleaning them out, the cost was 10 — 100 times that of getting the same yield from a field of corn. Is this going to be the same sort of situation?

HEDEN. The first person who has done detailed calculations, which I think permit some hopefulness for the future — they were published in 1968 — is Ostwald in Berkeley and there has been some later progress. Ostwald has been working on a sewage system. They have very shallow circular sewage ponds, and keep the organisms (a mixture of *Chlorella* and *Scene-desmus*) in suspension by slow continuous mixing at only 1/10 foot per second, interspersed for 1 to 2 hours every day with rapid mixing at 1 to 2 feet per second. This improves the economy, I believe. It has been tested as a fodder at the University of California at Davis, with good success as far as I can understand.†

WADDINGTON. Carl, you're putting this forward on the basis of its importance for feeding the developing countries, and that's certainly a strong argument. But I'd like to refer to the situation of the developed countries – actually I think some of them will be the first people who will be forced to exploit single-cell proteins and such things. At the present time, the traditional diet of the developed Western countries is becoming more and more dependent on high-protein animal food stuffs, mostly imported from developing countries with protein-starved populations. British culture is based on starting the day with a solid breakfast of bacon and egg. The Americans may be content with waffles and maple syrup, but there's often a pork sausage or two hidden in the pile of waffles. And of course the French have their funny habits, which we English refer to as 'a roll, in bed, with honey', but they make up for it when it comes to *dejeuner*.

But all the dairy, beef, pork, bacon, table poultry, and egg industries of the West are based on converting – very efficiently, let's concede them – protein-containing materials into other protein-containing materials which are both easily digestible and pleasant. This would be fine, except that in Europe – though less so in the United States – much of animal foodstuffs are imported from countries which need the protein much more than we do. Denmark, the country which has specialized most thoroughly on this biological conversion industry, at present imports about ten times as much protein per head of its population as a Dane eats of truly indigenous protein.† As for myself, I find it difficult to believe that this sort of thing can continue more than another ten to fifteen years. Take the estimate that, unless something radical is done *fast*, there will be 500 million to 1,000 million deaths from malnutrition in the world in the twenty years from 1975 1995. Spread evenly through the period, that would be, on the low estimate, 25 million a year, 2 million a month, half a million a week. Just how nice is your breakfast egg going to taste, if you know it's just a 40 per cent efficient conversion of food-stuffs out of their mouths? And, more down to earth, what is the price of cattle-cake, fish-meal, and so on, going to be? I think that Western protein-importing countries would be well advised to get going now, fast and massively, on developing ways of growing their own animal protein food-stuffs, from their own sunlight, even if, at today's prices, it's definitely uneconomic. In ten to fifteen years time, it will probably be the only possible salvation of what we accept as our 'standard of living'.

WADDINGTON. All those points we have been raising are points of bio-engineering. Working on them appeals to the type of scientist who has a practical bent. What are you feeling about the implications of these types of problems for raising fundamental questions that would appeal to the more academic-minded biologist? It normally is the case that practical applications do raise fundamental problems. I think nitrogen fixation and photosynthesis are both at the stage at which pretty fundamental considerations are absolutely necessary for much progress.

HEDEN. I don't know of any area where there are no factors which would stimulate a basic scientist. If you take an area like methane fermentation as one example, this is a very difficult matter. Many scientists have been looking at it, just as we do in my own lab, because it is such an interesting model. This is perhaps not basic science, but as far as the intellectual challenge goes it could easily compete, I think. Mass-transfer, electron transport, and genetic regulation weave quite a complex fabric which must be pierced before you can get at the practical solution inside.

WADDINGTON. I am asking this of course because of the present climate of opinion in science, the terrific esteem in the scientific profession for fundamental science, as opposed to more applied science. If one wants to get a lot of people to work in these areas one can rely to some extent on public spirit, and a wish to do something which is useful, but this would be reinforced if they were also doing something which was getting to the depths of biology.

HEDEN. I think the time is now right for creating forward-looking prizes, like a new kind of Nobel prize. I think there should be large awards for certain specified developments. Each time a prize is given — a quarter-million dollars or something like that — for an achievement which I would call a 'social invention' — it might be a scientific, a sociological, or a political invention — any time one gives the prize one should announce with a lot of publicity the target for the next prize. The needs in different parts of the world vary, so there should be five or six regional prizes and each year one would be given, so that the award could circulate. Of course, many people will have bad enough judgment to think that they might get the prize, so large numbers of people would flock into these areas and you would get a lot of work done.

MEAD. I want to say something a little tangential to this, about the whole relation between the very active application of science and when a basic scientist comes to feel depleted. They certainly felt depleted during World War II. Rabi wrote an article just after it, of the scientist returning to his dusty desk; he had only been applying the things he knew, and there had been no advances. This was equally true in anthropology. You get a sense of overdraft, and quite a kick into going back into basic work. Now, if we plan on a long-time basis, we ought to have some programmed plan, which might include things like the prizes that Carl is thinking of, that would create a kind of rhythm, so that people would work, say, for five years in applied work, and then have a right to work freely on whatever interests them most. The right to work at a top laboratory at a fundamental problem, if you earned it, would be worth more than a quarter of a million dollars, maybe — especially to young scientists in the emerging countries. You might transform your Nobel Prize in this way, or include some such scheme as this in some other of your plans.

HEDEN. This is an aspect which has been emphasized very strongly by Abdus Salam, who runs the Institute for Advanced Physics in Trieste. He claims that a major function of this Institute has been to provide a breathing space for students from poor countries.† They come here for a couple of months every year for many years and know that they have their chance to enter an intellectual community for a while and this is enough to stop the brain drain.

MEAD. I see *that* as the Prize, as it were; and you have to work for it. It would emphasize that you do not go into applied research to stay there forever, and become separated from your fundamental science. I think there is a genuine psychological feeling of depletion after a while. Things go too fast, you are using other people's basic science, you are preoccupied with bio-engineering or social engineering, and you get out of the feel of basic science, and this creates the awful gap between the basic and applied scientist.

PLATT. It's partly a fake, the lament of the scientists who went into World War II and felt that they weren't advancing basic science at all. As a matter of fact, World War II advanced physics at a fantastic rate. Within three years after the war you got the nuclear shell model, you got the meson, you got the hyper-fine structure of the Lamb shift, you got the invention of the maser and radio-astronomy. Many of these were made possible only by wartime apparatus, inventions, and measurements.

MEAD. I don't think it's fake, John. I think it's a genuine feeling. I wasn't talking about it being a fact, but I was talking about it's being a feeling.

SAGER. Pasteur, who was an applied biologist, revolutionized biology, but that doesn't make the people who work in applied biology feel so. I know you can't tell basic and applied science, one from the other intellectually, the only way you can tell is by how it *feels* and by that you can.

WADDINGTON. I am afraid, Margaret, I do think it is quite largely fake and this I think is what Gunther Stent is saying. There is a fearful lot of biology which has now got the charismatic title of 'fundamental', which is actually no more intellectually exciting than a lot of stuff which is labelled 'applied'. The really fundamental stuff is the work which changes one's basic ideas. In molecular biology there have been a number of really *fundamental* ideas in the true meaning of the word, but a terrific lot of molecular biology today is really no more than bio-engineering, and feels like it — there is the same pressure to produce results quickly, even some of the same secrecy in case you are scooped by some 'competitor'.

Before we stop I want to remind you that we have only touched on a few aspects of the possible applications of far-out biology. We have dealt mainly with food production, and hardly at all with population control or other aspects of human biology. And, within the field of food production, we have spent most of the time on Carl's fascinating microbiological stories. They are perhaps the most exciting, but they are not the whole story. We mentioned the recent successes of plant breeding. Now it's worth remembering that we are just seeing over the horizon the possibility for animal breeders to do one of the things which plant breeders have been doing for ages — transferring one or more chromosomes from one species to another, for instance, to bring in disease resistance or some such factor. We now have fairly reliable techniques for fusing cells of two animal species; we know that such cells often suffer mitotic disturbances, and that it is sometimes possible to select resulting cells which have most of their chromosomes from one species, but a few from the other — people have already made strains of human cells with one or two mouse chromosomes.† There is no difficulty in principle in injecting such nuclei into enucleated eggs, and rearing the aneuploid hybrid offspring — we could do it tomorrow with amphibia; we haven't yet got the techniques in mammals, but there are a few — a very few — people working on it. But this sort of thing — putting a horse chromosome into a zebra, and so on — might eventually yield a very big dividend. All our main domestic livestock now were tamed in the Neolithic — it seems about time we got ourselves something better for the less conventional agricultural regions of the world.

That is just one example. There are hosts of others. For instance, in many parts of the world, anything between 30 and 60 per cent of the crops which ripen in the fields get eaten by insects or other pests before they reach any man's table; not to speak of the losses that these same enemies of mankind bring about between sowing and harvest. We all know something of both the successes and the dangers of controlling these pests by poisons, such as DDT and others. But we are now in sight of much more subtle methods of control, by influencing the behaviour of the pest animals, either to lure them into traps, or to disrupt their normal reproductive or developmental processes in ways which are very specific to the particular species we wish to eradicate.† Many of these processes are controlled by specific hormones, or by scented substances ('pheromones'). The study of the ways in which these materials act not only would be of great practical importance, but should give a lot of insight into one of the most fundamental and mysterious problems in biology — the connecting links between the chemistry of the nervous system and an animal's behaviour. These raise very profound questions about the mechanisms underlying animal behaviour. Similar things occur not only in insects, but in mammals and birds.

There is a whole enormous range of topics in biology in which matters of great practical importance for society are intimately intermingled with the most fundamental problems. The arbiters of fashion in biology have singled out only a few of them, for instance, plant viruses, which are a 'respectable' subject both to agriculturalists and to the most upstage molecular biologists. What we need is that more biologists with influence, or more irrepressible young men, should get up and insist on the importance of the many, many more fields which could pay off as handsomely in both the 'practical' and the 'fundamental' currencies.†

But now it's time to adjourn for tequila and dinner.

*Towards a Post-Industrial World*

The situation and our understanding, values, and action
The end of Faustian man and the limits of progress
Biology and education for the future

## The Situation and our Understanding, Values and Action

PLATT. We must not underestimate the importance of the kind of flash of understanding which permits a person to restructure his own internal hierarchies, his own system of internal values, his own relation to the external world. And after the flash he becomes a different person. One sees this in religious conversion, one sees it in falling in love, one sees it sometimes in political conversions. Saul becomes Paul. The whole structure of the world is changed.

Now I think we are in the midst of a kind of collective flash of understanding for the human race as a whole, in which our hierarchies, or traditional ways of doing things, our feedback loops and lock-ins are going to be restructured into a world order, if we survive. Our business, it seems to me, as intellectuals, is to make this flash of understanding easier, and to make it more probable that we will survive as we go through the transition. What life will be like after this I am not sure. I agree with Stent in this instance that we are at the end of something, we are at the end of our old ways of doing and seeing, and studying science. I suspect that after this flash of understanding we will have entirely new ways which we can hardly foresee at the present time. But I think that the flash of understanding is a unique event in history — a milestone of thought — and will not recur for a very long time.

MEAD. In order to deal with any of our problems we need to have some sort of a mental picture of them — either a theoretical or mathematical model, or even a more elaborate simulation, for instance, by a computer. It seems to me particularly important now, when the main problems are world problems, that we should develop means of always also simulating the largest system we know when we are working on a small system, and always including the unknown as well as the known. These would be, so far as I know, new forms of simulation. There is no adequate planetary simulation at present. It is very difficult to think about the whole planet without getting confused. But the fact that the development of electronic powers of simulation have coincided with the recognition of the problems that face us should be treated as fortunate.

WADDINGTON. I am not certain I would not settle for something a little less than incorporating the total planet in every analytical small-scale operation. What I think does need to be incorporated is not so much an idea about the planet as a whole, but an idea about the situation as a whole. That is to say, an idea about the *whole* individual entity, that is interacting with its immediate neighbours, and about the *whole* of them. We tend to think of interactions of one person A with persons B, C, and D, and in this interaction person A enters as a fraction of himself, say as an administrator, or as a bank clerk, or as some other specialized function, but not as the whole of himself. And people he is dealing with also interact as only parts of themselves, as subordinates in the administrative hierarchy, or as customers at the desk in the bank.

I should like to change our approach so that we always think in terms of models which involve interactions between one whole person and other whole persons, not just between those fractions of the persons which seem most immediately relevant. Now, the full wholeness of any person does involve a reference to the planet – all right. But I think if you concentrate on bringing in the reference to the planet right at the beginning of your scheme, you may find yourself in effect taking a fractional view of the people, and jumping right from that to the planetary view, really leaving out the whole person which is in the centre between these two extremes.

MEAD. I am not arguing for a minute that when you want to analyze a small system you jump from the small system to the planet. What I am proposing is that at each point you can look at the superordinate system adequately, and there is no neighbourhood today, and no interaction between a bank clerk and his companion clerks, which does not include television news from around the world, and battles on the other side of the world, and Hong Kong 'flu', and we tend to leave these out all the time. When we specify the situation it doesn't make any difference how moral we are, if we leave out the fact of what they saw and heard that day.

WADDINGTON. I have a feeling that at present the world has lost a sense of unity at almost all scales, from the individual through these intermediate neighbourhood groupings right up to the world scale. The question is, do you need to recreate the sense of unity? And how do you recreate this sense? One of the ways to start is from the world scale, the global unity; another way to start is, of course, from the individual.

CAGE. I don't find the notion of unity . . .

WADDINGTON. I should not have said 'unity'; I should have said 'wholeness'.

CAGE. Well how was it that you should have said wholeness and you did say unity? (Laughter) I have been thinking about this question of unity and multiplicity, and for myself I prefer multiplicity. It seems to me to conform more with our circumstances than unity does.

WADDINGTON. Unity was a mistake, come on to wholeness.

CAGE. But the mistake is very revealing. Wholeness – the only objection I can see to wholeness is that it suggests that there are boundaries to the whole, and then wholeness is like unity. I would rather have 'open-ness', not unity or wholeness but open-ness. And open-ness particularly to things with which I am unfamiliar. I think that in society the stranger has always had a great integrating effect.

MEAD. Unless he's killed.

CAGE. But even if he is killed, perhaps. Henry Karl, for instance, used to explain the development of scales in music by the fact that a group would have, say, only two tones, and then a stranger would come bringing a new tone, and this would bring about an enlargement of the scale.

MEAD. If you consider the origin of language, different groups probably had different sets of sounds, which may have been largely instinctive, and it was bringing them into contact with each other, and somebody learning the other set of sounds, that made language develop.

CAGE. If one compares, for instance, the music of Bach and Mozart, you can take a small section of Bach and all the voices in the music will be observing the same kind of movement. That is to say, if the movement is chromatic all of the voices will be moving so; or if the unit or the module is rhythmically the sixteenth note, then if you add up all the voices you get a steady movement to the sixteenth note. This brings about a state of 'wholeness' or 'unity'. Which is a great contrast to Mozart. In Mozart, taking just a small section of the music, you are very apt to see not one scale, but I would myself see three. You would see one of the large steps made by arpeggiation of the chords; you know – thirds and fourths; then you would see diatonic scales, making use of the combination of whole steps and half steps; and you would also see chromatic passages; all within a small area sequence. They would generally be going together so that you have differences working together, in Mozart's case, to produce what you might call a harmonious wholeness.

But with new changes in music – those that we have had recently – we no longer see the coming together of disparate things as requiring harmony. In fact if harmony is required or imposed by the composer, it acts in our ears now to obscure the differences of the individual sounds. For instance, in Indian music, to hold improvisation together and to make it meaningful to the society, there were several devices – there was the drone, so that one could measure the different pitches with respect to this constant drone; and you could measure the time with respect to the unstated but understood drum beats. We are now capable, as musicians, of hearing *any* sound in *any* combination. The first musician to announce this possibility, by the way, was Debussy, already over 50 years ago.

WADDINGTON. You used the phrase 'to hold these things together'. I can't expound this in terms of music, but this raises a very general question, which I can put from the biological side. For instance, in a cell you have a hundred different things going on, but in the biological systems selected by natural selection, they all converge on a 'centre of attraction' as it were – they converge on a centre which somehow operates so that whatever comes in (or almost whatever comes in) you will get more or less the same coherent result. This is what I call a *chreod*.†

I wonder whether your idea of the human personality is like that? There are two alternatives: either a person is aware of everything that's going on as an individual thing unrelated to anything else; or he sees each thing as being in relation to other things, so that it is incorporated into a complex rather than being left isolated. I am putting this question from the point of view of someone who believes in organization, but you might express it quite differently if you don't believe in organization. This is the really general point I want to put to you, and you can express it in terms of music or in any other terms.

CAGE. Well, I believe in *dis*organization. But I don't see that in terms of non-participation or isolation, but rather precisely as a complete participation.

STENT. You, Wad, think that organization makes it easier to be part of a whole, whereas I believe that John Cage thinks it is an obstacle to becoming whole, because organization will create boundaries.

CAGE. Those rules of order must have been put there in order, as we say, to hold things together. Now, when they are taken away – if we take them away and don't have them – we discover that things get along perfectly well.

WADDINGTON. It is clear surely that, at the present time, we still have a lot of rules, put together in the past to hold things in order, and that these are no longer relevant. One of the major tasks of the present time is to explore things that fall outside the rules of order. But I am not convinced that this is a permanent situation. I think this anarchy that John Cage is preaching is really a sort of upside-down version of the American dream – which has turned out to be, in practice, a dream of the freedom and self-sufficiency of the individual as a competitive acquisitive operator. The ideal is to be 'open', in John's sense, but open to grab an opportunity. John wants the freedom and self-sufficiency of the individual to experience rather than to acquire. But, moving among all these public utilities – cars you pick up and drop as and when required, dwellings you go into and quit as you might a telephone booth – the person would be free but remain an isolated unit; none of the things he uses would belong to him, or connect him to anyone else, they would be socially as neutral as the air we breathe or the piped water we drink. I think biology shows that human life needs more social integration than that. After all, even as individuals we are not merely open to experiences, but have a central nervous system which is concerned with integrating those experiences. Perhaps the values John is advocating are the ones we need most at present, but in the long run we shall have not to maximize them, but to optimize them in respect to a system which involves social living together. I should like to go back to Margaret's point about the necessity for the individual to have some concept of the world as a whole. If one admits that at the present time what we need is freedom of expression, freedom of experience, and the ability to be aware of things that fall outside the accepted rules – from a long-term point of view, is this more than a temporary phase? Eventually you want to be able to be aware of these novel approaches, but aware of them not as isolated individual new off-beat experiences, but as things related in some way to a whole.

HEDEN. Isn't it important to consider, as far as the individual goes, two elements? There is the satisfaction of knowledge and doing – that is one fundamental factor. The other consists of functions associated with group survival. So there is, on the one hand, purpose, and on the other hand there is identification. I think it is very important that we should make limited use of the satisfaction of belonging to groups; because today many of our problems arise from the fact that we are deriving satisfaction from belonging to groups, which then enter into conflict. This is why I want to emphasize that we should concentrate more on professional functions than on geographical groups or communities.

I think world man is a very fundamental concept, and, as far as I am concerned, world man is of two sorts: one is the young generation, which has an acute global awareness; the other is the scientist, who gets his knowledge from an international storehouse, as it were. However, those two groups would be quite insignificant if they weren't subconsciously augmented by large segments of the rest of the population. Everyone who makes use of international air lines, or transport and communication companies, subconsciously realizes that he is part of a global culture.

SAGER. I should like to say that I think there are immediate goals for an affluent society. I think they are both realizable goals, and that they are also in a sense acceptable goals. They are short-run in relation to the kinds of things we have been talking about, but they do represent the next step, and they do represent perhaps a way of meeting this imminent catastrophe. They are goals which I believe have meaning to the generation we are worrying about, and also have meaning to our generation. There is the obvious goal of creating a world society which is a world *affluent* society; that is, solving the immediate problems of this acquisitive society, and the obvious inequalities and impediments to life for the majority

31

of the people on the planet. This is an immediate and not a long-range goal, in the sense that it does not deal with this issue of diversity, and 'what is the good life', and problems of that kind, but I think that they can only be approached stepwise.

Second, then, is the goal of a social consciousness which is real and legitimate, and able to relieve us of much of this frustration we feel and inability to find oneself and to know what to do with oneself. There are obvious immediate tasks for everyone who is willing to devote himself, but they are tasks which do not fit into the existing hierarchy of what is a suitable profession or how to earn a living. Joining the Peace Corps, or doing Peace-Corps-like activities, is not any sort of profession for a student, and does not provide a way of life indefinitely, or provide a source of income indefinitely. Nevertheless, it represents a model of what many people would like to do for a considerable length of time. It is a model which is really appealing to a large number of young people, who join the Peace Corps for many other reasons besides avoiding the draft. So I feel optimistic in the short run as well as in the long run; if there were only some way of coping with these paralyzing official government social forms which simply block you every inch of the way! In this sense I am very much in sympathy with 'copping-out', a total rejection. I think this is a symbolic thing; it doesn't mean that we are going to cop-out of the world and die of starvation. It is just that we refuse to accept the things that are being demanded of us, because we think that if we do accept them, then we are trapped by what we don't want; so we will *reject* until those consequences and relations are broken down, and it becomes possible to reorganize things – and *fast*. I think that this demand for instantaneous change is fitting.

WADDINGTON. How far is this copping-out on a protest about material things like inequalities of wealth? I should have thought that was not probably the most important thing. We are certainly moving towards an affluent society, though we haven't quite got there. There are anomalies, the ghettos, and so on, which really have got to be put right – but those aren't the only problems. Isn't the important thing today rather the impersonality, the lack of participation, the frustration of individual development? . . .

SAGER. I think you are wrong in trying to deal with these things separately. The practical problems you mention are often a product of impersonality. There is today a sense of alienation – you are prevented from doing something which is demanded by your moral principles and the things you believe in, which you are not allowed to express. For instance, something like half the population of the world is now living on sub-standard diets.

MEAD. But most of the young people of the world are not so much concerned about that half, they are worrying about the meaninglessness of their *own* lives.

HEDEN. I wouldn't agree with you on that. In Sweden they are worrying about undeveloped countries too. When you have reached the affluent society locally, which you could do perhaps by putting in the bulldozers and rebuilding the ghettos, then the next step for the young generation to focus on will be these issues. The fact that we Scandinavians can concentrate on them now is because these other problems aren't quite so bad for us.

WADDINGTON. I think it is significant that Marcuse writing about 'The Escape from the Affluent Society', in a book which seems to be widely influential among young people, did not say anything about the non-affluent parts of present society, but argued that even if society is affluent we still want to escape from it. I think this is more fundamental, personally.

SAGER. I found that very unsatisfactory myself.

MEAD. But the kids don't. They admire it.

HEDEN. They need purpose, I think this is the key word here. In different communities it will certainly be formulated in different ways.

MEAD. I agree with that. They need purpose, and they are living in a society where the transmission of *commitment* has broken down. If you look at the 1950s in the USA – and we have looked at it in considerable detail – in the 1950s the same young people, from the same kinds of families and with the same education, had just one aim in life, which was to get married, move to the suburbs, get a nice house and a station wagon and four children. They didn't have a purpose that they were sufficiently caught up in, so they did what was expected of them without worrying very much about purpose. Now this all shifted within a decade. In about 1960, due to a whole series of things, we had the birth of a search for a more adequate purpose than the perpetuation of the society. If you are in a very affluent society you do not want to perpetuate it, and if you are in a very poor society you don't want to perpetuate that. It is a bid against mere perpetuation and for more consciousness – for more consciously informed involvement, I would say. It occurs in every country in different ways.

SAGER. Wealth is not the point. I don't see Margaret's argument as in disagreement with what I am saying, but I feel very strongly that the emphasis, at least of many of the young people whom I know, is an emphasis on frustration. It's not that it is an affluent society; it's a paralyzing society. And part of that paralysis comes from them having this world view, this recognition that the world is affluent here and starving there, while they cannot express themselves in effective action. Part of the reason they cannot express themselves is a kind of feeling of moral shame. I think that until that is cleaned up it is rather foolish to think in terms of aims beyond that, or goals beyond that. That represents the first step that one has to do something about.

WADDINGTON. Ruth, I can't really agree with you on this — I'm more on Margaret's side. The poverty of the developing world *can't* be the fault of the new generation, they just weren't around early enough in history. It is the fault of anyone in the Western world, it is of us, and of our parents and grandparents. We were undoubtedly guilty of stupidity — putting too much effort into medicine and saving life instead of into agriculture and nurturing life, which has given us the population explosion; trusting too much in phoney economic theories about trade, and developing agriculture for export cash crops, not for the basic local necessities. And, let's face it, we were guilty of the straight exploitation of natural resources, thinking that if our technology allowed us to discover oil in someone else's country, and our capital let us produce and refine it, then we had the right to most of the resulting wealth.

Our only defence against this last charge is to argue that the developing countries might not have done much better! If you want to see a modern distribution of natural wealth which is, in world terms, really crazy, visit an oil-rich under-populated Sheikdom on the Persian Gulf, and then an oil-poor over-populated Arab country like Egypt. Or, to take other examples, visit a palace or even a tomb, of the Moghul Emperors of India — Amber or the Taj Mahal — or the Imperial City and the Ming Tombs in Peking — or, for that matter, walk a few hundred yards up the road into the Chichen Itza site, and look at the Castillo Pyramid and the Ball Court — and reflect on what the Hindu, Chinese and Mayan peasants might have done with that wealth. These things are beautiful visually, but they're ugly socially.

But, leaving these local situations, I want to get back to my major point. Which is — the affluent countries *cannot* fully solve the problems of the developing world. Not because of lack of wealth — we certainly ought to be providing them with at least ten times as much as we are doing. But because these people need to, and want to, solve their problems themselves. Not only materially, but they have also to change a lot of their social structure and traditional ways of life, and this they *have* to do for themselves. We can't and we shouldn't intrude too much. The main job of our young generation in this connection is to see that we don't stand in their way — as we so often have done — and that we give them what help they responsibly ask for.

But, isn't making this *the* central issue in the dissatisfaction of the affluent young perhaps merely finding, ingeniously, a scapegoat which allows you to avoid facing up to the real issue, which is a tougher intellectual and moral nut to crack — namely, what should be the quality and character of life in an affluent world? What I think the West has to do now is to produce a way of life, based on technologically-achieved wealth, which is *good* enough for you to offer it confidently to the poor parts of the world, as something which they might consider imitating, or at least getting on a level with in their own characteristic way. All we offer them now, by way of example, is an invitation to come and join our rat race.

John Cage, you said that the devil in your world is power, and you talked about hope – you used the word 'hope' – for overcoming it. Platt said 'work for overcoming it' and you rather repudiated work. This raises the question of dealing with power not by power but by some means other than power. I think this is one of the key issues. You can try to deal with power by copping-out, or by retreating into drugs or hippie-behaviour, but unless *everybody* does this you merely concentrate the power into the hands of the people who don't do it. It doesn't remove their power. I think this is an important problem. What does one do? Ghandi did it – his passive resistance was one way of controlling power by something which itself is not power.

CAGE. I agree actually with 'work', against power, but after all the effort that has been done so far . . . the urgency of the situation makes it look ineffective. Well, we continue, but it is with hope, and something like desperation begins to come in.

My notion of how to proceed in a society to bring about change is not to protest the thing which is evil, but rather to let it die its own death. And I think we can state that the power-structure is dying because it cannot make any inspiring statements about what it is doing. I think that protests about these things, contrary to what has been said, will give it the kind of life that a fire is given when you fan it, and that it would be best to ignore it, put your attention elsewhere, take actions of another kind of a positive nature, rather than to continue to give life to the negative by negating it.

The summer before last, I organized a group, much on the lines of this group, in New York – all sorts of people who were at one time engaged in protest. I asked them to discuss, once a week through the summer – what one could do to change society, other than to protest it. There were some 12–20 people at each meeting, so there were many minds, many sets of experiences – and the only solutions we could all agree upon were the projects and works of Buckminster Fuller.

This is something which is coexistent with the evil. The technology is developing in spite of, or at least coexistent with, the power and profit structures.

WADDINGTON. This meeting here was also called to discuss something which is coexistent with the evils but is quite separate.

CAGE. Right.

WADDINGTON. I mean the ideas from biology, the ideas of organization, and participation, of optimization rather than

35

maximization, and so on. I don't say that the biological movement is yet as powerful and well worked out as the Bucky Fuller one, but it is something of the same kind.

CAGE. You know about Bucky's so-called *World Game* 'to make the world work'? This would be in computers with teams playing against one another. The idea is to see how we could make plans whereby everyone in the world gets what he needs from the world's stockpile of available resources. This calls upon the technology which is developing in spite of or at least coexistent with the power and profit structure.

HEDEN. I want to come in with a cynical remark. If we scientists were all New York longshoremen there would be no problem. We would have solved the world's problems in a hurry. If scientists were only as aggressive as longshoremen!

WADDINGTON. We should have gone on strike?

HEDEN. We should have formed a union, sure, there is no question. That's the only thing the politicians understand. We can talk our heads off about non-violence, non-power, and so forth. The only communication link with the political decision-makers is the impact of coordinated efforts involving large numbers of people.

WADDINGTON. I think the two most significant things that have emerged in this discussion are two rather paradoxical ones. John Cage, who, more than any of the rest of us, lives a life focussed on the creation of works which appeal to the whole man in his full humanness, has come out with the idea that from his point of view the great dominating influence is technology — the technology most fully formulated by Buckminster Fuller, but in which all of us socially-conscious scientists are also engaged to some extent. And then the most technological person here, Carl Heden, professionally an industrial microbiologist, weighs in with the thought that the scientist and technologist needs to come out of his scientific-technological shell and start operating — positively and aggressively — in the fields of politics and trades unions. Both of them see the main problems of the world today as being on the other side of the artificial fences we put up around particular domains of human interest. They are not, I think, just trying to pass the buck to someone else. What I gather from what they are saying is that the acute problems of the world can be solved only by *whole* men, not by people who refuse to be, publicly, anything more than a technologist, or a pure scientist, or an artist. In the world of today you have got to be everything or you are going to be nothing.

## The End of Faustian Man and the Limits of Progress

STENT. 'Faustian Man' strives for power over his environment; but the achieving of power is satiating, and will (in 30 years?) turn off the drive. The accelerating rate of progress means that

36

we must approach certain limits (for example, of air transport) in a few decades. So the twenty-first century will be hippie, Polynesian, non-striving. (The Beatles and the Beatniks are the first symptom.)

Limits of progress have been reached *now*, in Arts and Sciences, for a similar reason in both cases.

CAGE. Progress may be the idea of *dominating* nature. But in the arts, it may be *listening* to nature. In the forties, I conceived the idea of a piece *with no sounds in it*, but I thought it would be incomprehensible in the European context. Five years later, I was inspired to do it by seeing the paintings of Robert Rauschenberg† — one of which was a canvas with no paint on it. Charles Ives† wrote a romantic essay about sitting in a rocking chair, watching the sunset, 'listening to your own symphony'.

MEAD. As in a Quaker meeting.

WADDINGTON. I remember in a Quaker meeting in my childhood listening to the bees.

CAGE. I once went to a Quaker meeting — with silence — and found myself thinking of what I should *say* — that is, how to dominate the meeting (Faustian!) — and then I realized that was not the point — not to dominate, but to listen. And to listen to silence. By silence, I mean the multiplicity of activity that constantly surrounds us. We call it 'silence' because it is free of *our* activity. It does not correspond to ideas of order or expressive feeling — they lead to order and expression, but when they do, it 'deafens' us to the sounds themselves.

WADDINGTON. Your silence, Cage, is an instruction to listen. An art object is always an *instruction*, to do or to experience, not a piece of information; and living things are organized instructions, not organized information.

SAGER. What the kids are disgusted with is domination. I would emphasize the coming of understanding — intellectual and sensual.

CAGE. One of the things we *don't* need as much as we use it is *memory*.

WADDINGTON. What Cage is pointing out are the misuses . . . The intellectual mind is a dangerous organ, like all organs . . . He is emphasizing the positive value of what is better called 'mindlessness'.

CAGE. Or '*fluency* of the *mind*' . . . Those 'ruts' (self-reinforcing loops) should not develop; they should remain open to experience.

PLATT. Is not this a necessary historical process? We have studied the world analytically for 2000 years, like taking a watch apart; and finally we will want to put it together again so it works like a watch. (to Mead) Sorry to use a mechanical example, but we can't yet take a frog apart and put him back together.

WADDINGTON. Yes, there can be reaggregation of cells in a frog — at least up to a certain stage of development.

PLATT. The frog cells reaggregate and make a whole frog again because (1) each of the cells is a wholistic system, complete in itself to a large degree, not 'cut up'; and (2) each of themselves has internalized the information — the principles of the whole system. Analogy: to make a whole interacting world, we need the principles of structure and interaction of the world to be internalized in each of us — so that when we meet each other our interaction is consistent with the interaction the world must be built of.

MEAD. What you call 'Children of the Universe' in your book, *The Step to Man*.

WADDINGTON. If you experience anything for the first time with no 'curtain of memory over it' (as Duchamp† said), you no longer have power or domination over it. Organization in the biological world — and in the physical world too, for that matter — arises not from relations of domination, but from relation of 'participation'. Everything we give a name to is constituted by its participation with everything else and by everything else's participation with it ... The quantum physicist has to say this — and calls it interaction. Whitehead used the word 'prehension' — essentially the same idea I call participation or involvement ... To some young people today participation simply means being a full member of the committee, with all the voting rights; to others it means something more like an intimate involvement in deciding and carrying out, together, whatever is going on — a sort of 'I am you, and you are me' set-up with others in the group. I am using it in the second sense. When Whitehead says that a thing we give a name to is a 'prehension', he means that it is most usefully regarded as the sum total of the participations, in this sense, of that thing with everything else in the universe.

A cell is the *involvement* of enzymes with each other. Sure, it is *causal*, but in many different ways. A word like 'involvement' gives the idea of the multiplicity of kinds of causes. It is the same for an organism; the same for society.

MEAD. This idea has often been expressed in various different ways in Oriental thought.

STENT. (coming back to the main argument) Scientific disciplines are *bounded*; that is they *are complete*, like geography.

WADDINGTON. (interrupting) Geography complete! Ask a modern town or regional planner, it's the most open-ended subject going.

STENT. (continuing) Genetics is bounded; also biology; also chemistry ... Not because we have understood everything in these fields, but because we can now imagine what it would be like *if* we knew everything.

Physics is *not* bounded; it deals with fundamentals. (Therefore we cannot say what it would be like to know new fundamentals?)

Unique events are not science. Mandelbrot† speaks of this as the first kind of indeterminacy — events with which one can deal only statistically ... Uniqueness equals 'noise'. *An ensemble of events, each of which is completely unique, is perceived as noise.*

Some fields of physical science are even more difficult because there are no *mean values*, such as in meteorology and some branches of hydrodynamics ... This is the rule in social sciences. This is the second stage of indeterminacy, where we can see some structure, but it is hard to predict because things are jumping around all the time. We must deal with such areas *impressionistically*.

MEAD. (interrupts to criticize Mandelbrot's ideas) Most economists never approach an event, or a human being, directly. They are two degrees away from taking scientific data.

WADDINGTON. One name for this meeting would be, 'Biology and the History of the Future' because history is unique. There is a difference between prediction and explanation. History is concerned with *understanding after the event, understanding the nature of the set-up not the details.*

There are many types of breakdown of chreods† (stable patterns): for example, waves turning; jets of water breaking into drops ... The range of mountains breaking up into peaks. All these are non-predictable but understandable. (Cast a glance over your shoulder at Alfred Jarry's Dada Science — Pataphysics,† the science of the unique event, the science of imaginary solutions.)

SAGER. Counter-example (to Stent). Karl Marx developed a profound theory for the description of society (even with all its errors), which could not be done by the kind of method used in the physical sciences. A good intuitive theory tells you what to look for ...

MEAD. The difference between science and engineering is that the scientist can *never* tell you whether the bridge is going to stand-up — against rust, tropical rain, the habits of the natives. If the bridge breaks, that doesn't mean the theory of bridges is wrong. The fact that social science can't predict exactly what we should do doesn't mean that it is not science.

WADDINGTON. Science has been concerned with those parts of the world we can take into the laboratory and analyze. A lot of the world we cannot take in — events that happen only once, that are too big, and so on. That doesn't mean we can't treat them by science.

SAGER. Verifiability in complex fields helps *illuminate* the world, helps you understand ...

WADDINGTON. I don't just want to be 'illuminated'. I want to *deal* with the world ... In non-laminar flow, one can probably never predict every flow line, but we *can* build planes and submarines.

MEAD. When Marx made an initial statement, it was probably not much more important than Newton's – but it *was* that important! It gave a basis for taking data and building the next step.

WADDINGTON. The exponentially accelerating rate of change in the world means that effectively Marx is nearly as far in the past as Newton. What we are involved in is not any sort of once-off revolution – though something like it may be necessary in some places to burst open locked doors – but very rapidly and *continuously* accelerating changes in many aspects of society.

Going back to Gunther's point, if you took the statistics of the consequences of moving the pawns on a chessboard, it probably would not converge to a mean value (not a Mandelbrot distribution?), but that does not prevent some people from being good chess players!

STENT. (quoting his brother-in-law, who is a champion) In 1928, Chess Theory came to an end with Capablanca; today the theory is no different. Chess has become a psychodrama, of psychological dominance. Now, the Masters can't even formalize their own skills; you can't program a computer to do it like them, because they don't know what to tell the computer.

What will the future be like (if there is no nuclear holocaust)? Gabor has emphasized an increase in leisure, and argued that this will be a major problem, but leisure is only a problem to 'Faustian' man. There have been many leisure societies; and the rise of Beat philosophies today means that we are approaching one.

MEAD. 'Leisure' is a silly Puritanical term. 'Leisure' is when you are not working and getting ready to do some more work . . . We should forget the word – in good 'work' you don't know whether it is 'work' or 'play'.

STENT. The Beats gave up the idea of fulfilment through action, but they still relied on external inputs (sensations). The Hippies go further, and repudiate the external world altogether, giving internal inputs (dreams, perhaps induced by drugs) the same value as external inputs. That's as far as you can go.

MEAD. It would be wrong to compare the Hippies with the Polynesians. There were no Polynesians that didn't work – none that lived on a 'remittance man's' check. But the Beatniks and the Hippies today are supported by their parents. In Polynesia, everyone had a social responsibility and everybody worked (for a short period each day), perhaps more like our future society; supported in their case, as in ours, by a blessed economy.

Polynesian societies had fairly beneficient salubrious islands, but they also developed homicide, murder, cannibalism, warfare.

The New Zealand Polynesians (Maori) actually provisioned their war parties with human victims. Why should you believe that this idea 'We aren't going anywhere anymore' will actually happen? It has never occurred in human history before . . .

The Northwest Coast of America offers a much better example than Polynesia. In three days a year they acquired their principal food supply (salmon), then they built, carved, danced, were active . . . In fact, there is no evidence that 'leisure' has ever been *bad* for human beings.

STENT. I see a tripartite society of the future, with something like 'α's, β's, and γ's'. So we can say several things: the average distribution will be much less 'gung ho', much less 'driven'. But at one extreme end of the spectrum will be those interested in machines and power. They will keep the machines running. In the middle, a *Beat Group* will be 'transcendental', or impressionistic; customers for 'action paintings', say. And at the other extreme are Hippies, who will be the drop-outs, the internal vision people.†

PLATT. We will *all* do this, each one playing every role — but at different times of day!

WADDINGTON. 'Beatniks' are just 'the other side' of power. They are excess manpower in a society which has plenty of worthwhile, in fact essential, things to do (rebuilding our cities, to start with), but no way of getting this sort of capital investment actually carried out.

MEAD. We know one primitive society that had hoboes (the Manus of New Guinea). The hoboes came in canoes, not walking; but they had to chop wood for their supper — and this is a society that had enuresis and neuroses, and all the symptoms of power-pursuit.

PLATT. (a note) Stent said he hadn't thought about the 'generation gap' or social directions of science until a good girl graduate student told him she was dropping out. He tried to persuade her not to, with the usual arguments — that she should get her PhD first, that then she could get a good job, and so on. But she just sat and laughed at him for his assumptions. And convinced him *his* motivations — for getting out another paper, climbing academically, keeping at work 'for the excitement of the scientific work' — were no more worthy or well-considered than those of a Wall Street stock manipulator. That 'it was time to live — to get out of the up-tight, Puritan society, to let it go hang so as to be yourself'.

And this forced him to a profound and long rethinking of his motives, and of where science was going — and he made a nuisance of himself at parties, criticizing the scientific venture and its assumptions (until his wife protested that he was driving away all their friends). But he was then asked to give the Berkeley lecture series, with a year off to prepare them, and so came to write the seven chapters of his book, *The Golden Age*.

PLATT. In dealing with social affairs, we are handling *systems*. Good example of a system — developing a weapon-system, for example, fighter planes in the Korean War; the problem was: how many enemy planes shot down, per own planes lost? (to be maximized by adjusting speed, armour, firepower, ground cover, and so on).

A system has a boundary, with high internal interactions and low interactions across the boundary.

The present world is not a system, but a *collision* of systems. We need to work out a new kind of interaction between systems to produce a stable global organism into which the smaller systems have been incorporated.

WADDINGTON. We are like a primitive cell which first comes across a bacterium which will be later taken into it as a mitochrondrion!

PLATT. The way to produce a viable design for a higher grade organism is to build up 'lock-ins'. Examples of locked-in systems — the President, Wall Street, industrial-military complex and the political opposition, in the US: Again — every little college in the US, started *any* way, turns into a four-year liberal arts college. Hutchins tried differently, and was shot down, and Chicago College became almost the same kind in just a few years.

WADDINGTON. 'Lock-in' is an unattractive metaphor. It suggests a set of a smallish number of rigid cogwheels which cannot get out of mesh with each other. A similar, but biologically-derived idea is a 'chreod',† very many components, related every way in a network of interactions, to produce some stability of the pathway of change as time passes. In a social lock-in each component tries to maximize its own gain; in a social chreod each component tries to optimize itself so as to maximize the global goals of the system as a whole.

SAGER. Do we want stable systems, whether lock-in or chreodic?

PLATT. A malfunctioning self-stabilizing system can be corrected only by the intervention of a system of higher order.

MEAD. The higher order system may be acephalous, not centralized.

CAGE. I don't especially want to be forced to drive on either the left or the right, as one seems to be forced to do with these 'lock-ins'. Several years ago, I enjoyed riding over the mountains in a jeep, because it could go anywhere. I enjoyed the non-locked-in character of the Japanese language as distinguished from the locked-in English.

MEAD. But in the flexible Japanese or Chinese language, you can't tell direction precisely, so that your jeep can't even *find* the back of the mountain. Without exact structure, you can't even make a jeep.

But I think Platt's metaphor is too mechanical, too hostile. It suggests a prison.

The biological term 'chreod' or canalization of the course along which a system develops is much more appropriate to bring out the value of organization.

PLATT. I *am* hostile to some lock-ins. I want to know how to change *those*, but then I want to know how to establish others that give useful structures.

WADDINGTON. The possibilities of 'chreodic alternatives' should be produced from within us — not imposed from without.

PLATT. There are eras when men have too much fluidity and invent structure — and others, like ours, that are over-structured, and want to explore more fluidity ... The time required for the adoption of a major social invention is about the same as for a technological invention — say fifteen years.

WADDINGTON. Operational research (cf. the Korean War example that Platt mentioned) was invented in Britain about 1939, and in full use by the end of 1940, under the urgency of war.

PLATT. The next twenty years of history should be treated with the urgency of a war.

MEAD. Permissive child care came in five years, after the 1930s.

WADDINGTON. Biological chreods are only stable within certain limits, and normally break up after a time. René Thom† calls the break-up points *catastrophes*, and has given the mathematical theory of them; there are only seven possible spontaneous types of catastrophe. In the development of a biological organism, an early chreod breaks up into two or three others — that is, the early embryonic cells become differentiated into more fully developed types — liver, muscle, kidney, and so on — for which new control systems, of hormones, nerves, and so on come into play. We should try to design more fully developed social systems into which our existing ones can switch over.

PLATT. One higher type of system would be to go over from 'zero-sum games' — what you lose, I gain — to 'non-zero-sum' games, like Prisoners' Dilemma [WADDINGTON. (interjecting) Another unappetising name!], in which the total gain to both players is great if they cooperate, but each has a *chance* of a bigger gain if he is uncooperative.†

'Bootstrapping', society raising itself from within, without anything being imposed from outside.

CAGE. Lock-ins and bootstrapping are 'thing' notions, not 'process' notions. What is outside the system? Where is the Nothing-in-Between (the component systems). If the system (or systems) is periodic, any aperiodic event disturbs the periodicity; but in a chaotic array, the addition of periodic events does not disturb the chaos. Nature is aperiodic; our notions of order are elementary compared with Nature's.

WADDINGTON. Arp,† in his Dada days around 1920, wrote

about his art works, 'These works, like nature, were ordered "according to the laws of chance", chance being for me merely a limited part of an unfathomable *raison d'etre*, of an order inaccessible in its totality'. And Schroedinger† defined life as based on 'an aperiodic crystal'.

CAGE. Why do we need order? You gave the reason, so that people don't kill each other. That is, what we want is for *people* to live, not the *system* to live. Thoreau's anarchy (he quotes, e.e. cummings†)

> O sweet spontaneous
> earth how often
> has the naughty thumb
> of science prodded
> thy
> > beauty
> > . . . . . .
> > thou answerest
> them only with
> spring

When I was growing up, Church and Sunday School became devoid of anything one needed . . . The public schools avoided such 'needs', and what I was forced to do in school was what I no longer wished to do – including Shakespeare. I was almost forty years old before I discovered what I needed – in Oriental thought. It occupied all of my free time (aside from musical work) in the form of reading and attending classes of Suzuki† for several years. I was starved – I was thirsty. These things had all been in the Protestant Church, but they had been there in a form in which I couldn't use them.

MEAD. Yes, the thought of the Protestant and Catholic Church was not really available to the young, which is why so many turned to Zen.

CAGE. Jesus' saying 'Leave thy Father and Mother' meant 'Leave whatever is *closest* to you'. In Zen, one speaks of 'non-minded-ness'. The idea of Nirvana is not a negative statement, but the 'blowing-out' of what is seen as an impediment to enlightenment. The ego is seen as the one barrier to experience. Our experience, whether it comes from the outside or from the inside, must be able to 'flow through'. Irrationality, or 'non-mindedness', is seen as a *positive* goal, which is *in accord with* the environment.

MEAD. It is wrong to call this 'unreason'.

CAGE. But poets, experimenters with madness, came out of an over-rational culture.

MEAD. But what comes out of dreams and art is as valid a contribution as so-called 'rational thought' . . . A 'cosmic sense' is as necessary to being a man as breathing; if you don't put something in, you don't get something out . . .

Madness *is* interesting; there is something there. But you also get much from poetry, ritual, art; but don't call that something irrational.

CAGE. We are interested in *something more* than the gathering of information.

WADDINGTON. Putting down (writing) what you understand is a different process from seeing what you can understand . . . But this 'mindlessness' seems to me like being a vegetable. I'm sure *you* don't mean that, but you haven't made clear how it is different.

CAGE. In Zen meditation, it is important *not* to go to sleep, not to be a vegetable. Awareness is not vegetation. If you become something through which experience can flow, your inside is also the outside . . . Here is another use of the rational mind that is objectionable: You hear a sound; you think it is 'A', and then you think it is 'not a very good A'; and yet there are *many kinds* of 'A'.

MEAD. Zen is one of the antidotes we have brought in from another culture . . . A new kind of awareness, but to call it irrationality is wrong.

SAGER. But it *is* irrationality; it is a refusal to deal with the issue.

WADDINGTON. I agree, it is an attempt to deny that the world has a structure — which is, basically, a causal structure. Now that structure isn't the whole thing; but you cannot be aware of the whole unless you are aware, to some extent, of the structural elements.

CAGE. Technological achievements should not *determine* what we do, but they should be *utilities, channels*, through which we express whatever we want to.

WADDINGTON. There are public utilities in the body — nerves, blood vessels . . .

CAGE. Would you say the body is nothing but utilities? . . . The publishing of music is oppressed by 'middlemen' who are *not* open channels but are determining what gets published.

WADDINGTON. The biological model of society is really not an organism but an eco-system. There are no 'middlemen' in an eco-system, but each component is interacting directly with other components.

CAGE. The telephone system is not a 'system of systems', but a *utility*. We need to make our utilities functional throughout the world. We should want our organizations to *allow things to happen* (and *more* things than otherwise, without organization), but they should not determine *what* happens.

When I dial, I want to *get what I expect to get*. But in my music I want *space for surprise*. I want us not to be inhabitants, but tourists, meeting new experiences; drawn to them (as we are here at this meeting in Mexico).

My attention was attracted to the 'x-quantities' — to the things *outside* of formal teaching — to the innovative things.

MEAD. You dislike governments; but we have got to survive.

45

CAGE. The idea of world structures is a beautiful picture, but I don't want governments to control our lives.

PLATT. But with *limited resources*, we *need* mutual control.

MEAD. We can't have *everybody* tourists. Then there would be none of these 2000-year structured cultures to visit.

CAGE. (*re*: living together under rules) I would rather see a society with individual murders than with international murdering.

WADDINGTON. Anarchy demands *a space* to be anarchic in. You can't have a (safe) playground without a fence around it.

CAGE. I want the police *not* to control traffic of private cars, but to maintain a fleet of communal cars that we can use when we need, and leave when we are through . . .

I agree with McLuhan's idea† that electronics has extended the central nervous system, and that this network is now becoming a world mind; and that the new psychoanalysis is to deal with the malfunctions of this *world mind* . . .

I am wondering about the necessity of expressing a thought, since this thought is usually already in the world mind. When I express what is a new idea to me, I often find later that someone else has already said it.

We need to move from a fixed view to a larger view, such as George Mead's,† which pictures man belonging to a family, city, nation, and world; then in a religious view, belonging to everything.

When I first began to work on 'chance operations', I had the musical values of the twentieth century. That is, two tones should (in the twentieth century) be 2nds and 7ths, the octaves being dull and old-fashioned. But when I wrote *The Cycle of Changes*, derived by chance operations from the *I-Ching*,† I had ideas in my head as to what would happen in working out this process (which took about nine months). They didn't happen! − things happened which were not stylish to happen, such as *5ths* and *octaves*. But I accepted them, admitting I was '*not in charge*' but was '*ready to be changed*' *by what I was doing*.

So I want to give up the traditional view that art is a means of self-expression, for the view that art is a means of self-alteration, and what it alters is *mind*, and mind is in the world and is a social fact . . . We will change *beautifully* if we *accept* uncertainties of change; and this should affect any planning. This is a *value*.

HEDEN. The point is to maximize choice, by making many differentiated societies.

CAGE. If you maximize choices, you will go on choosing as before. The point is to increase willingness to accept what happens.

In reading about the future, we read we may 'lose *privacy*', which is taken as a value. I question whether we ought to consider privacy any longer as a value; rather *getting together* is a value, and enjoying each other.

WADDINGTON. Cage is suggesting the values of the 'interstices' in the culture — of the *free areas*.

CAGE. I think the idea of 'rights' belongs to the world of possessions. We want to get away from the 'rights' to something freer.

MEAD. The only cultures that have made *all* the adults 'equivalent' to parents are artificial societies — The Hutterites, the Kibbutz, the artificial world of *Walden Two*.

PLATT. Some *minimum* right of privacy, but also some *minimum* right of human interaction is necessary for healthy biology (as some minimum right to maternal care in infancy).

MEAD. I would like to emphasize *'self-optimizing* people' instead of *'self-maximizing people'*. 'Maximizing' is of one or a few variables; while 'optimizing' is for the purpose of the whole system.

SAGER. I don't think the 'will to power' is just 'The Myth of Sisyphus', letting the stone roll back so that you will have something to do.

Domination of nature is not the problem any more. The motive is *understanding*; and understanding without fear. The rebelling students don't want to fall into this trap, of the dominations and fears that have not worked.

What is needed is a *new ideology*. Many are scared of knowledge because they don't know where it will lead (work on viruses, episomes and so on has military BW applications).

We need a new *feeling of confidence*. 'Prisoners Dilemma is liberating; it gives a new vision of what might be done.

For the feeling of individual worth, dignity, and power, we need a more normal, less neurotic, psychology. We need to see that individual psychology has to be understood in terms of interpersonal relations and social role. People need to feel confidence in their *creativity*.

WADDINGTON. The most important biological value, evolutionary potential — the sort of thing that would give you confidence to be sure you had -- is not a quantity of some definite characteristic, like intelligence, or 'fitness', but is the ability to find some way of fitting into, and making a go of, anything that may turn up — a new ice age, a new disease, or predator. This is what young people need to have, going into the future.

SAGER. The main problem is to convey motivation, and then show the real basis for optimism There is a failure to convey a framework for constructive thinking.

MEAD. Motivation is not something that can be conveyed. You cannot motivate people — the idea is taken over from the manipulation of experimental animals by reinforcing particular inherited trends. Human 'motivation' cannot be handled in this way. We should look at the behaviour of people, and consider how to elicit its strength. In the USA during the

Berlin crisis of 1961 when Kennedy called for individual air-raid shelters, the healthiest children were those who had parents working on something for peace or for civil defence, admitting the danger but doing something about it.

STENT. Is motivation a useful concept in handling choices?

MEAD. No, the proper concept is *character*, which determines how individuals and members of different cultures will choose. But I agree with Ruth on the importance of having a world view within which you work. This can bring people's own intrinsic powers to life. Utopian visions – and nightmares – can be important components in choice.

Culture is within the realm of biology. It is a form of human adaptation, as biological as the pattern of a bird flying home to his nest, although the learned components predominate.

Our culture in the past has depended on growing up in a three-generation community, in a particular spot. Since language was invented, men have known about other groups, because of adopted children, intermarriages, extruding exiles into other communities, and so on; and so they have learned about *other* cultures. Later, there came migration on a large scale. Children born in new places were 'natives', adults moving to a new place were not. This has been the rule of change – the mechanism of cultural change for thousands of years.

But, with formal schooling we have changed the method of transmission of culture. Before, most learning was inarticulate. The baby 'taught' the adult – to nurse and care for a baby reared in the same cultural system is a self-reinforcing, self-teaching system. But today, as it has been said, this is the first generation that has been reared by the mass media.

So in the schools it used to be that teachers or priests had grown up in the system – and so they could teach their own and other people's children what it had meant to grow up in a certain way.

Today, we have *no* adults who grew up in the system they are attempting to teach, manage, interpret, and work with! Nowhere in this earth (including New-Guinea-people with transistors listening to space flights) are there such adults!

*Today, all adults are immigrants in the Post World War II world; it is the children that are the natives.*

What the generation gap is, in deepest meaning, is that *for the first time in history the young will not wait*. We always said, 'Wait, in twenty years you will be where we are and can take over'. Now they feel the people in charge are not to be trusted, are not natives, do not understand the country. They do not think it is safe to wait.

This is the first time in history that this has happened.

Nevertheless, the adults will not abdicate. So we need a *completely new concept of communication,* across a gulf greater than trying to move from one culture to another. It is a great gulf; and the youngsters best adjusted today are the children of the people who were forerunners of the present world.

The content (Maoism, Democratic liberalism or something else in different countries) is irrelevant to what I am talking about — regardless of content, the fabric of transmission has been terribly torn.

PLATT. They *know* more than we do.

MEAD. But *we also* know more, in certain fields, where experience matters. The problem is to bring these different kinds of knowledge together.

What we have today is 'a peer-group culture' teaching each other, and it is like two people trying to make love who have never made love before, and they are poor at it.

The young and the old together must build the new things that need to be built.

We need a mechanism by which the new learning, which they have sucked in from birth, can be added to the knowledge of the old.

SAGER. What can they *not* learn from each other?

MEAD. How to change! This is what the old know ... We have lived through the greatest changes ever yet experienced ... This is what the old have to teach. The young see the adults as having failed at managing the world, but *we* have to teach them enough about change that they will have the flexibility they will need.

WADDINGTON. And how to arrest change, or at least guide it. You can't go blindly up an exponential increase in things indefinitely. At some level of population numbers, we'll all just be putting our sewage into each other's drinking water, as Carl Heden points out. At some level of speed of aircraft, they go into orbit or take off into space. We're not very far from those limits. The young generation, or the next after them, will have to learn to get progress under control again. They'll have to learn to assess priorities; among the almost infinite range of things they *could* do, they'll have to decide which they *want* to do. The old have had experience of deciding how to lay out their meagre resources to attain the goals they thought most worthwhile; the middle group have all the resources they wanted, and no real constraints on how they used them; the young will have such abundant resources that the plethora of things they could do will face them again with a need to *choose*. The forty-five-year-old parents of today's students don't know much about choosing, but the pre-World War II generation had to do a lot of it, though, I admit, in rather different circumstances than those in which our students will have to choose.

STENT. What about making a living?

MEAD. That's no problem in the US. It is easy with our affluence, too easy. The result is that these young of ours don't know what to say to those trying and needing to make a living in developing nations. Those of us who know we are in a new world can teach *that* to the children ... We need to *include* all those who have been 'objects', to whom things have been done, children, patients, medical students, subordinates. They need to be able to contribute what they know.

We need to change from transmission to transaction. Transmission is for slowly-changing societies. Transaction is necessary for fast ones. We need to make this change in our 'transmission' methods for at least several generations ahead, as the changes continue. But today the young may feel so distrustful and alienated that they may do nothing but smash; and the old, with guns, only suppress ... But we won't have another chance. One can't let this happen.

WADDINGTON. In my book, *The Ethical Animal*, I argued that the main advance of the human world over the merely biological is that man has, in effect, got himself a second, and much more effective, genetical system by developing language as a way of passing things on to later generations. I claimed that in order for this to work, the young babies have come to realize that some sounds are *words*, with meanings, not mere noises; and this, I thought, in practice involves an acceptance of parental authority in controlling the child's behaviour. It is from this acceptance of authority that the whole notion of the ethical, of things being right or wrong, and of there being goals beyond immediate enjoyment, really arises. I wonder what happens to ethics, and goals, if the whole idea of authority breaks down? Perhaps it can't break down that early in life, when babies are first learning that there is such a thing as language. Anyway, as I also argued, in the past it has nearly always been hideously exaggerated, and led to much too rigid ethical codes, and the Super-Ego, and so on. Perhaps we can hope now, in a less authoritarian world, to find it easier to get a decent Ego without too dominating a Super-Ego.

MEAD. We need a new locus of authority, not the kind of parent or teacher who says: 'I'm your parent and I tell you to ...' This is an abuse of biological parenthood. We need to say, 'I will *never* order you to do anything just because I am your father; never the unnecessary, the frivolous or trivial. When I speak, it will be because I am, at that moment, responsible.'

We must resign all the superordinate positions associated with *status*, and replace them by those associated simply with greater knowledge (or experience). In such a system, the group itself, young and old, builds its own rules ...

The main reason for emphasizing child care today is that it alters adults, not that it alters children! It alters them as parents, teachers, supervisors.

I'm not sure the younger generation has moral *consciousness* that we can depend on. They see our hypocrisy, but there is no real authority, no anchorage, for the values they proclaim. No parents, not the past, no God, no book, no vision of mankind, and they see no reason for a waiting period, for capital accumulation, for work, and so on ... There is instant rising expectation; and they don't see why everybody shouldn't have *at once* what they see on TV. The young communists of the '30s valued things in terms of the future, but they don't now.

WADDINGTON. Auden expressed the '30s feeling in 'Spain':†

Tomorrow, perhaps the future. The research on fatigue
And the movements of packers; the gradual exploring of
    all the
    Octaves of radiation;
Tomorrow the enlarging of consciousness by diet and
    breathing.

Today the deliberate increase in the chances of death
The conscious acceptance of guilt in the necessary murder;
    Today the expending of powers
On the flat ephemeral pamphlet and the boring meeting.

The stars are dead. The animals will not look.
We are left alone with our day, and the time is short, and
    History to the defeated
May say Alas but cannot help nor pardon.

SAGER. But this student demand (*Now*) is right!

PLATT. We *are* able to get the bulldozers into the ghetto tomorrow morning, if we are fighting a war! We just don't believe it is that urgent; and the young see that we don't.

WADDINGTON. There are two very peculiar things in 'The New Morality' with some of the students. (1) Total anti-intellectualism — rejection of rationality as such; and (2) politics of confrontation, where the aim is to drive the situation to a breakdown — an 'orgasm' — a much deeper anarchy than John Cage's, not aiming at an anarchic Paradise, an anarchic Garden of Eden, but at *breaking things*.

MEAD. The notion that it will pay to break up the system has been living on as a residue of the age of faith. It is acting out, and reacting to, what is left of the old values.

WADDINGTON. In *The Ethical Animal*, I said that one of the great dangers was having any *single* system of values. We need at least two systems 'at right angles to each other', complementary to each other, like particle and wave in physics.

## Biology and Education For The Future

SAGER. In terms of our role as educators in this changing society, we need to concentrate on helping the critical people, that is, those who are in college now. What I would like to ask is: what do you think anybody who is entering college now should learn? If you were going to college now, what would you really want to know?

CAGE. I think a class, or whatever you want to call it, in what Buckminster Fuller calls Comprehensive Design Science, is essential. That means not studying something in a form isolated from everything else.

PAPAIOANNOU. This is what we try to do in our courses in Ekistics. I would say — without promoting one or the other, whether it is general design science, or whether it's ekistics — the general educational programme for anyone entering college should contribute to the formation of a generalist, so that they will acquire a perspective on a number of more general problems as well as the specialized ones that they select.

WADDINGTON. I think the essential point about the generalist one wants to produce by education is an interest in the future. What is majorly wrong with our educational system at present is that students are taught *nothing* about what is likely to happen in their lifetime. They have to invent all this for themselves. We have already mentioned the point that they have to be educated for being able to accommodate change. We can't tell them what is going to happen in their lifetime, nobody knows. But they can be taught to think about it, and to be ready to deal with it when it appears. This means, I think, a very much more profound generalism than is usually considered. It really means basic philosophies, values, types of concepts. I think it is essential they should be given a Heraclidan view, that the world is a world of processes and is not a Democritean world of things, because they are going to be immersed in a flux of process. But in their normal scientific education, all the stress is on things.

HEDEN. There are now several independent and strong pressures towards something called a World University.† In fact, Buckminster Fuller's group, through John McHale, forms one of the first centres in a 'faculty' tentatively called Comprehensive Planning. I think that making education international, or regional at least, from the very start is fundamental. The students have to be brought out of their immediate environment in a most direct fashion. One of the World University concepts is that the students, to get a degree, would have to combine training in different centres. Considering the possibilities we have now and will have increasingly of transporting students or faculty, it is quite within the range of possibilities to establish a roving kind of structure. This is essential if we really want to make use of the feeling that most students have for international trends. It falls in with their concepts of world unity.

CAGE. We want to see the world as a university from which we never graduate. This trend is already showing. In the mid-West, and I am sure in many other places, they have what they call a mid-Western complex of universities, and a student can take advantage of the services of any of those placed and still be effectively in his own university or his Alma Mater. In other words, I think the notion of Alma Mater ought to give way to just 'world'.

PLATT. Could I say a long word for a minute or so about what I see as the structure of universities that we are moving to? I have a little lecture that amuses some people, it's called 'The University is a Five-Legged Animal'. I'm afraid though that it's not very biological. The left hind leg is scholarship, a knowledge of the past, of history, of everything that men have known; the left front leg is teaching, the transmission of this to the younger generation; the right hind leg is creation, creative research in science or new creations in art, music or literature, or the discovery of new ideas. The right front leg is public service, that is to say, it is using these general ideas, this repository of knowledge, for the general public. This includes government and industrial consulting, as well as other forms — in these days it's coming to be mainly urban affairs. But there is still a fifth leg. When giving the lecture I wait to see what people will think the fifth leg will be, then I hasten to reassure the ladies in the audience that this is the elephant's trunk, which is reaching forward to a grasp on the future. This is innovation. By this I mean not merely the public service that government and industry know they want, but the creation of new concepts, new principles, that government and industry don't even know they want. This would include atom bombs, it would include oral contraceptives, or things like the Gallup Poll or Keynsian economics — things which change all of society because they are so deep and fundamental.

WADDINGTON. It should include not only technological things, like atom bombs and Gallup Polls, but also conceptual theoretical ideas — new types of thought. It should include the kind of considerations we have been spending time on — ideas like the value of silence, of mindlessness — these are new ideas and value systems. A worthwhile university should be considering ideas of this kind in relation to the future, just as much as improvements in video telephones, or other technological developments. But one of the characteristics of existing universities is that they *do* contain creative scientists but do not on the whole contain creative writers, poets, artists, or musicians.

PLATT. I want to claim that a university is incomplete unless it has these five functions in some degree. Now if you look around you will see that most universities do not have these five functions adequately. Either they go in for teaching and neglect research, or they have lots of research and neglect the teaching, or they have lots of government service in Washington and neglect the fundamental innovations, including the philosophical innovations. What we need to have, as a kind of brain of mankind, must be simultaneously a knowledge centre, *and* a creative centre, *and* a decision centre, *and* an innovation centre, as well as a transmitting centre. There are only two or three universities that have all these functions complete — there's Harvard, or the Harvard—MIT complex, and a few others. The reasons why the European universities are falling behind in their influence on European society is because they do not have the public service and the innovative function nearly strong enough. They are still too heavily weighted towards scholarship of the past.

CAGE. I think the various conventional forms that afflict the university at the present time should be bypassed, or steps should be taken to remove them. For instance, I was once talking with Varese on the subject of harmony, which now takes a year to be taught in a university. We both agreed that anything useful about harmony could be taught in one half hour.

WADDINGTON. One thing about the great advances of science, they enable you to get rid of much of the detail. Once you have got a real genuine understanding that the genetic material is DNA, you can forget a vast amount of experimental work that was preparing for this generalization. The information explosion should not lead us to think that knowledge is becoming unmanageable, because it is combined with an understanding explosion, which makes it comprehensible again.

CAGE. You have to be careful, when discarding ideas which have led to some final generalization, that they don't also point in other directions, which were not followed up. I don't think we understand anything unless ... I'll put it affirmatively. We understand things by means of what we do. That is to say, without doing *something* we tend to be blind to everything, but the moment we do do something that action opens our vision to the things in the past and the things in the future. By doing, I mean making something or creating something, or devoting ourselves to something. That act enables us to see other things. When we say that such and such a thing is a generalization or a conclusion, it is because what we are doing enables us to see it as such; but if we did something else, we might see some of the things that we thought were of no importance as being extremely interesting. I spent many, many years finding the music of Charles Ives of no use, and then, because of changes in my own music, Ives became of paramount importance to me.

WADDINGTON. I should like to go back again to what this curriculum is to consist of. We have said it will have a strong flavour of innovation and study of the future, but it's got to have some real factual things in it. Now part of the reason for calling this meeting together, of course, was to say that biology, in the general sense that we have been discussing it, is one of the basic elements that should go in the curriculum, both from the point of view of practical affairs, such as Carl was talking about, and from the more philosophical ideas of participation, organization by optimizing instead of maximizing the sub-entities, and, of course, from the fact that in discussing man we are essentially dealing with the development of a biological organism into a component of a social system. I think that any educated person capable of dealing with the future has to have a certain amount of basic biological understanding. He doesn't need to know precisely where the various arteries go, what the hormones do, and so on, but he does need some general ideas about the nature of biological systems.

PLATT. There are two general things we should teach. One is chain reactions, and the other is cybernetics. I am shocked at finding seniors in the university who know nothing about either of these, although they are the most important general ideas of the last thirty years. The reason is that they don't belong to any course, they don't belong to physics, they don't belong to chemistry, or biology, or psychology, or economics, although they have been seminal ideas in all of these field.

HEDEN. Human ecology from the group psychology point of view would be extremely important. I would like at this point to cite a little piece out of 'Wasteland culture'† which I found thought-provoking. The author talks about a man by the name of Caplow, who puts it 'that "status" is what is central to the idea of human organization'. Then he asks: why? 'Because the more status the less it is necessary to rely on human interaction and personal relationships. When people communicate too much the prestige and power of the superior drops. Moreover, organization is coterminous with compulsion; where compulsion does not exist organization is impossible and where compulsion is unnecessary, organization is also not required'. This is a condensed statement of a rather baffling argument.

WADDINGTON. I profoundly disagree with it, as I'm sure you do. Organization does *not* depend on compulsion. The most typical place to find organization is in the biological world. There is no compulsion within an embryo which organizes it. There is a human idea of organization, drawn from the model of the army or the church. It is a totally non-biological type of organization. Biological organization, as I have said earlier, depends on participation between the components, which interact with one another in a very intimate way, so that you can't really separate them – when you do separate them logically, as separate components, you are bound to omit something of the way they interact with one another. It's not clear that anything made of a lot of interacting or mutually participating components will *automatically* become organized. In the biological case, natural selection has picked out the

55

right sort of components, so that they do become organized. I think that what Caplow says is just exactly what we want to fight against, that organization can happen only by compulsion.

HEDEN. What I wanted to imply by citing this is that this is the sort of problem, which should be brought before students. I called it group psychology, maybe human ecology would be better.

WADDINGTON. I should call it almost a problem in general philosophy. It is certainly the kind of thing that I think students ought to be aware of. It should be raised to students by lectures or by seminars, for them to discuss.

CAGE. I would suggest that instead of there being *required* studies, they should simply be made available, in an environment which is conducive to people becoming interested. The interest in such general questions should arise in the student, rather than being forced upon him. The reason I dropped out of college was because I was absolutely horrified by being in a class which had, say, 200 members, and an assignment being given to have all 200 people read the same book. I thought that if everyone read the same book it was a waste of people. It was sufficient for one person to read the book and then somehow through that person, if the book had anything in it, everyone could get it, by talking with the person who had read the book. But to look at those desks with everybody reading the same book, that struck me with horror, so I marched away and went into the stacks of the library. I read books as irrelevant to the subject as I could find, and when the questions were given for the examination, I got an A. I thought there was something wrong with that system, so I dropped out of college.

Now, the situation we have here right now, the discussion in this room, is an excellent one for education, and it also occurs, doesn't it, at the graduate level? Ought it not to seep down through and penetrate and characterize the whole university? That is to say, people coming together and exchanging their information; and then, through the (what?) *brushing* of their information together one with the other, stimulating further perhaps unwritten information. People acting together synergistically, rather than each one as in a factory doing exactly the same thing as the others.

SAGER. One asks a bit more of the university. One asks of the university assistance in structuring your acquisition of knowledge. When I came to college I wanted to know, what is there to know in the world? I am very grateful to the University of Chicago – there was one first year in which you could take all sorts of courses, which provided a survey of knowledge. After that at least I knew what was known, even if only in terms of broad subject matters, and I could go and carry on from there. But I needed this kind of syllabus and I don't see anything wrong with it. It didn't bother me a bit that 50 or 100 other people were doing the same thing at the same time, because everybody is entitled to know what there is (*John Cage*. Yes), so I felt that was all right. If you read Plato and enjoy it immensely, wouldn't you like someone else also to read it? And then you can discuss it on the basis of both having read it. I think that's more sensible.

CAGE. Yes, but I think this notion of a curriculum and practices such as having people read the same standard text are based on the conviction that at the basis of learning is language, which is understood by each person and that people would not be able to communicate unless they had the same information. Now, in the Arts at the present time, this is not what obtains. In your book about painting, Wad, you show that a painting is no longer just a surface with splendid interests, but is rather an overall situation – an experience which is not imposed by the painter on the observer, but rather is created by the observer in his use of the painting. Today, all through the world which uses modern art, what we have are *inter-media*. It is extremely common practice that many things go on at once. In a theatrical or musical or any such situation, the centre of interest is nowhere to be observed, it is interesting all over.

This means that the basic notion of an agreed-upon language is being given up. The characteristic of one of our events, that includes music, and action, and film, and slides, and so forth, and which is present in what we call serious art, and in rock and roll performances with films and stroboscopic lights, with dark light and all these things – the characteristic thing is that after two people have experienced it they would be able to converse and exchange their experiences, which have been *different*. I don't think syntax or language in a conventional sense took place. It is something far more all-pervasive which took place. Two people in such a situation, with the activity surrounding the audience, might have their backs to one another and literally see different complicated things, though they were present at the same event. And that is our life experience. Why are these arts the way they are? They are not that way in order to simply break the laws of art, they are rather that way in order to introduce us to the life we are leading, so that we can, as you say, participate in it.

I have from time to time, either for myself or for others, made statements that are like manifestos. You know this is popular in the field of the arts – to say in a manifesto-type statement what distinguishes the contemporary or modern thing from what isn't. The first time I was asked to do it, I did it with regard to painting. I said that a painting was modern if it was not interrupted by the effect of its environment – so that if shadows or spots or so forth fell on a painting and spoilt it, then it was not a modern painting, but if they fell on it and, so to speak, were fluent with it, then it was a modern painting.

Then, of course, I have said to you the same thing about music. If the music can accept ambient sounds and not be interrupted thereby, it's a modern piece of music. If, as with a composition of Beethoven, a baby crying, or someone in the audience coughing, interrupts the music, then we know that it isn't modern. I think that the present way of deciding whether something is useful as art is to ask whether it is interrupted by the actions of others, or whether it is fluent with the actions of others. What I have been saying is an extension of these notions out of the field of the material of the arts into what you might call the material of society. If, for instance, you made a structure of society which would be interrupted by the actions of people who were not in it, then it would not be the proper structure.

WADDINGTON. Your modern piece, in my terminology, is a chreod. It is a system which can absorb potentially disturbing elements. This is just what I mean by a chreod. But, I think you can push this too far as a quality belonging to *all* art which can be called modern. Certainly it is characteristic of one of the main – perhaps *the* main – types; that which stretches from Jackson Pollock and deKooning to Rauschenberg and Jasper Johns (but even there, was it so true of Rothko and Clyford Still, for example?) – and then on to the Happening boys. But what about the good Pop people – Lichtenstein, Warhol, Hockney? I'm doubtful of its relevance. And there is a whole movement, which I shouldn't hesitate to call 'modern' on something more than merely chronological grounds, to which it certainly does not apply – Hard Edge artists like Ellsworth Kelly or Richard Smith, sculptors like Anthony Caro, Phillip King, the middle Paolozzi – or again Op painters like Vassarely and Bridget Riley. There are *many* modern arts, as there are many modern sciences, which is just as well, and we can hardly be expected to content ourselves with just one.

But now let me go back a bit and point out, John (Cage) that in one of your earlier talks you said you had spent a year, or more than a year, studying Oriental thought and philosophy. This is not just reading one book about it. You went quite deeply into it. Now, possibly because of where it comes in most people's lifetime, the university conventionally is a place where people tend to want to go fairly deeply into something or another. They should be able to select what they go deeply into, and it might be a mixture of Oriental philosophy and bacterial genetics, or some other eccentric combination of disparate subjects, but it seems to me, there is an advantage in going deeply into *something*.

CAGE. I think that society, in one way or another, should recognize the value of doing this, but to have a large number of people going deeply into the same thing, not of their own will, but because it was considered good for them, is not going to accomplish that goal. When you said that a poet and artists, and so forth, should be in university communities, I think the advantage from that would be that by their activities the students would see that these people were *devoted* to what they were doing. I think that we study, we teach, throughout our lives, whether we hold classes or not, and we do it by this effective means of example.

SAGER. I want to discuss more fully and definitely the place which biology might have in university education. The over-riding problems that plague us today and may destroy us tomorrow must be solved not by future generations but by people already born. The college generation who are rebelling against the onrushing mad course of events represent key participants in the struggle to save mankind. Modern technology has eliminated war as a practicable basis for political rivalry, but the message has not been comprehended by the generals and the politicians. The use of war as an instrument of government continues in its central role. However, there is an increasing understanding by individuals throughout the world of the futility of war in the modern world, and as this understanding grows, we may anticipate that the mass base which supports warfare as a form of politics will crumble.

If the human race is not wiped out by warfare, we will have the chance to come to grips with our next most pressing problem: an equitable distribution of the world's goods and services to a population small enough to be well fed, clothed, sheltered, and educated on this planet, in a style consonant with human dignity, growth, and development.

This conference has dealt very little with politics *per se*, but not for reasons of blindness or political naivety. It has been our aim to explore activities that would contribute powerfully to strengthening individuals in their quest for a better life, anticipating that many of these activities could bypass conventional politics. An important feature of these activities, including educational ones, is their positive feedback: each success provides more strength and encouragement for the next step.

In all societies, the education of the young is based upon the values of the adults, their picture of the world, and their expectations of the lives their children will lead. Today we are in a period of such explosive change that adults cannot know for what sort of a life they are preparing the young.

Clearly, students throughout the world are beginning to see the inadequacies of traditional education and the values on which it is based, in training them for their future. There is no single or simple answer to this problem; nor can any one individual provide a general 'solution'. New educational aims have to develop in relation to new societal goals and understanding. In this sense, I think that the new educational patterns to be developed, far from being 'value-free', will be the expression of an emerging new value structure.

WADDINGTON. What I was getting at earlier was that with the increasing amount of leisure, people attending the university in the guise of students in the future are going to be not much different in age, if any, from those in the so-called faculty. This is bound to lead to a completely different structuring of university operations.

CAGE. I think that if we could give up the division between students and faculty, and do as Fuller has said, return the teacher to his studies, it would then be a simple matter for people in that situation to see that some were older, some were younger, and to connect with the older ones certain advantages and with the young ones others.

SAGER. A new code of values can be derived from concepts of physiological and psychological health (as best we can define them). In an attempt to define these values, I have codified my concepts of health into a Biological Bill of Rights for Mankind. I shall attempt to show that using this Bill of Rights as a guideline, one can generate a new sense of purposefulness and new lines of action for these times.

A Biological Bill of Rights for Mankind would be like this:

1. The right to an adequate food supply, free from toxic additives or pollutants.
2. The right to have clothing and shelter consonant with physiological and aesthetic requirements.
3. The right to live in an equitable physical environment, aesthetically attractive and physiologically healthful.
4. The right to an upbringing that does not emotionally malform, and does lay the basis for healthy psychological development.
5. The right to free education, continuing as desired throughout life. (The aim of education to be the growth and development of the individual to the fullest extent of capacity and desire.)
6. The right to live in an equitable psychological environment, characterized by respect for human dignity and diversity.
7. The opportunity for creative work and self-development at all stages of life.

Political theorists of the nineteenth century viewed the rights of man in terms of material security: food, clothing, and shelter; and this view remains at the core of present-day 'welfare' programmes, and indeed of Labour Governments and Welfare States. It is now becoming apparent that two psychological features are as fundamental as the physiological ones: concern for the dignity and sense of human worth of the individual; and assurance of help in finding an appropriate niche for self-expression and activity which would lead to self-esteem and the esteem of one's peers. If the central importance of a psychological sense of well-being were recognized in the evaluation of health, it would lead to fundamental revisions not only in the planning and execution of welfare plans but above all in man's perspective of a more equitable future.

The provisions in this Bill of Rights may appear Utopian in the context of the day's newspaper headlines, but they are not Utopian in a material or technological sense.

For the first time in recorded history, we have reached a technological level in which the potential for material security for all depends primarily on the *organization*, of production and distribution, rather than on the activities themselves, which are becoming ever more highly mechanized. Most technological surveys indicate that, at the present level of world population, there is enough manufacturing and agriculture potential to support everyone at a relatively high living standard. Of course this situation will change very rapidly if the population continues to increase. Thus population control and an equitable redistribution of the world's goods and services, including education, represent the urgent first order of business in the world today. Carrying this out in a constructive manner, not redistributing the *in*equities, should offer an adequate challenge to the most talented and sophisticated youth. Thus we have two fundamental differences from the past: the possibility of affluence for all, and the need for large numbers of people with highly trained and innovative minds.

At present, the world contains countries at every level of development with respect to material security: from the Scandinavian industrial-welfare states, to Western industrial societies like the United States with 'pockets of affluence' and 'pockets of poverty', and on to the underdeveloped countries with under-privileged populations, under-educated, under-nourished, and in some instances actually starving.

In his book, *The Golden Age*, Gunther Stent dismisses the problem of organizing a new social order with the assumption that it *will* come, willy-nilly − and then all the world's population will be in the same fix: affluent, secure, with no motivation and nothing to do. This problem is well known to designers of Utopias, but I do not consider the problem of motivation in this context as a serious one in the world today. In my view, the reorganization of society represents the core of the conflicts that we may expect during the rocky period from now to the twenty-first century. If there is any decay of motivation among young people today, I think it springs from a profound sense of confusion and frustration, not from a loss of drive or concern. The problems are very difficult and the solutions depend greatly on the wisdom of the youth of today who will be the principal protagonists in the struggles to come. What can we teach them? How can we help them?

The direction of change in education is towards occupations demanding imagination and judgment as well as knowledge and skill. One line of thought about the future has viewed the 'work' of society as a 'utility' to which everyone makes some contribution, possibly quite dull but short-term, while for the rest of the time he is free to do what he likes. There probably will always have to be some dull work of this sort, but already it is only a constantly shrinking fraction of the total activity. It seems likely that the principal occupations of the next few generations will be in teaching, in research, engineering, health and medicine, comprehensive design science, and services including town planning, architecture, construction and arts; in the distribution of goods and services; and in governance. These occupations have much in common, in providing scope for individual initiative, growth, and development. For people in these occupations, the distinction between work and play will tend to disappear, as it has already for most artists and scientists, and the 'problem' of leisure time activity will not arise. We may say that one aim of education is the development of individuals for whom leisure is no problem.

HEDEN. There is something which I do think we must remember, and that is that we all seem to agree that there is a certain elementary need for utilities — medical men who know how to operate on us, and a lot of other things like that. There will always have to be a lot of professionals for society's needs. They may, of course, also have a cultural interest. It is unfair to exclude them from this type of participation, which we essentially do if we overload them. Now, to make it possible for cultural involvement to embrace the whole of society I guess that you must require from every individual that he participates in meeting the technological needs.

CAGE. I agree completely.

WADDINGTON. I like this point that Carl made, that everybody should have something of utilitarian use to give to society — of course, 'utilitarian' includes writing poetry and painting pictures, it's not all a matter of the medical profession or the professional engineer or chemist — but I think this comes back again to the point I made about our present universities, that they don't contain the people who contribute to society by creation in the art and humanities field. If this was the form of utility you were providing, the teachers in the university have got to regard these as creative fields, not simply as fields of study, and have got to be creative themselves.

SAGER. Clarification of values and of educational aims should make it possible to restructure courses in a dramatic way, focussing them in a direction consonant both with student interests and societal needs. Within this general frame of reference, I would suggest the following four goals for college education at this time.

First, the student should be made aware of what is already known in the world: the extent of man's knowledge of himself, his physiology, his psychology, his relations with other individuals; modes of social, political, and economic organization present and past; the nature of the physical world and man's environment; and our cultural history.

Then he must be provided with methods, tools, and experience in the acquisition of new knowledge and the application of problem-solving techniques in each of several fields.

Then again the student should be helped to examine problem areas of the present world: social, political, technological, and conceptual; and to carry out an original research project in a chosen problem area.

Finally the student must develop his individual talents and find a niche in which to engage his energies constructively in the world and his college experience should assist him in this crucial task.

I would propose that such a college curriculum should consist of the following subjects:

1. World Civilization : a survey of the cultural history of mankind, including prehistory, primitive societies, Eastern as well as Western philosophies, technologies, aesthetics, creative achievements and disasters.

2. Biology and the Nature of Man.

3. The Physical Environment in which we live.

4. Human Ecology, man's relation to his environment.

5. The World Today : theories, data, empirical procedures of analysis to describe and to evaluate the social, political, and economic conditions of existing societies.

6. New Methods of Thinking and Problem-Solving : scientific attitude and scientific method : operations research ; new maths; computer logic and programming; cybernetics; game theory ; systems theory ; application of these methods to current problems of social organization and research.

The design of all these courses will require a fundamental rethinking and restructuring well beyond what is now being taught under these or similar headings. Introductory science courses have generally been designed to attract students into the profession, and so the approach has been pre-professional rather than educational in the broad sense, while science courses for non-science majors have tended to be watereddown versions of the pre-professional ones.

We need to do something totally different. We need to acquaint the student with science as a part of his cultural heritage.

Traditionally our cultural heritage has been viewed as the teachings of poets and philosophers, never of scientists. Indeed, many people confuse science with technology, an unfortunate and hazardous misunderstanding. The cultural heritage of science has three aspects: the scientific method, which is the process of making discoveries; scientific knowledge itself; and finally technology, which is the application of scientific knowledge to solving specific problems.

I would propose that the subject matter in the science courses be keyed into Human Ecology, which I see as a pivotal course in the curriculum, linking general education with practical applications and with the student's choice of an area of specialization. At present the trend in good science courses is to focus

63

on the 'hot' areas of current research; I would propose now to redirect the choice towards areas of current problems.

The course should certainly include considerations of population size and distribution, birth control, nutrition and dietary variations over the world, the planning of human settlements (ekistics), existing conditions of human life among under-privileged people (urban slums, rural slums, in the United States, Latin America, and the rest of the world), problems of pollution ( air, water, food, thermal, radiation ), conservation of natural resources, effects of noise, crowding, lack of privacy, the importance of beauty in the environment.

An essential prerequisite to the development of this sort of curriculum is a vastly increased and sustained concern for Human Ecology on the part of the faculty. So far as the science faculty is concerned, we are beginning to see increased activity at three levels.

1. Over the past twenty years we have seen spectacular advances in our understanding of fundamental processes in biology, especially in the molecular basis of genetic control and regulation of cell growth. With these powerful new understandings, it has become possible to attack many kinds of applied problems such as contraception, disease and public health, microbial food sources, and ecology with a new precision. As a result, applied problems have become more accessible to systematic investigation and more attractive to scientists. As interest rises, the status of applied research will rise, and more investigators will be attracted to these problems. Concomitantly, the image of a scientist as impersonal, austere, and unconcerned about the impact of his findings will change to an image more in keeping with reality.

2. There are also problems that require the joint action of scientists in groups. Two examples of this kind are the publication of the *Bulletin of Atomic Scientists*, now in its twenty-ninth year and the publication of the journal *Environment* ( formerly called *Scientist and Citizen* ) and other activities of the Scientists' Institute for Public Information.

As the deterioration of our environment proceeds at an accelerating rate, it has become evident that far more widespread, consolidated, and sustained efforts are necessary to inform and to influence the government and the public with respect to biological hazards in particular.

3. The emphasis on applied research and human ecology must be carefully balanced with the continuing drive for new knowledge, the continuing essential role of basic research. There is a great deal more to be known, and penetrating further into the secrets of life and the universe may provide new and fundamental solutions to existing problems. Man's curiosity and quest for knowledge is our most precious asset and must be nurtured at all times. As current crises loom, we must not forget that new discoveries may yet transform our problems

by providing radical solutions as yet undreamed of. To maintain a balanced perspective in the face of growing crises will require yet another kind of publicity and mass education. In the past it was customary for scientists to restrict the discussion of their research aims and results primarily to colleagues and students, often on the assumption that no one else was interested. Explanations of research goals and their significance were buried in grant proposals. Habits of communication between scientists and the public have hardly developed at all. The reticence of most scientists to talk freely in a popular vein about their research has not helped those few journalists who have the foresight and desire to write about basic science.

Now, almost suddenly, it has become apparent that communication between scientists and the world at large is highly desirable — even essential. Not only do scientists need the financial support of the government — ultimately of the public — but the long-range value of public understanding of science is daily becoming more evident. Thus, we need to open up new channels of communication and to develop new habits of communication. Popular writing, lecturing, interviews, and lab visits all represent important opportunities for scientists to explain themselves, their work, their goals, their enthusiasms, and hopefully to capture the imagination and interest as well as the support of the public.

At this conference, we anticipate that the critical problems of the next decades will be biological ones; and we propose that not only the knowledge to solve these problems, but also the values and the motivations behind our actions are themselves biological in content and significance. In this context, it is appropriate and necessary that biologists intervene increasingly and directly in problems of human ecology, and that they devote themselves increasingly as well to intensive education of the public in science for survival and science for pleasure.

WADDINGTON. Let me say one last word about universities and techniques of teaching. Just to remind you what a fantastically complex and difficult job we are asking them to do. John Platt said that they are five-legged creatures — scholarship, teaching, research, public affairs and innovation. Now they have in Britain somewhere around ten students per faculty member, or a bit more. In the United States, in Europe, usually a great many more. If the staff — or let's call them the permanent or semi-permanent residents at the university — are going to do all these five jobs, they are obviously not going to have a great deal of time to spend on any individual student. You may say, let's have some university staff mainly concerned with teaching and others with research or innovation and so on, but that's not really good enough.

The people the students want to meet and participate with are not only the good teachers, but also the good innovators, or researchers, or the people in contact with industry, government, and so on. Until the universities are given a great many more staff — which perhaps they will be, in a more leisurely time — there simply won't be enough man-power to make it possible to turn the whole teaching system into one depending on small informal discussion groups such as we have been having here. This may be — probably is — the best teaching method, but it is fearfully demanding on man-power and time. I think the best hope of getting towards it is to invest far more in students' libraries of films, video tapes, and all the other audio-visual aids and teaching machines we now have in addition to books, so that the students can do most of what is now course work in their own time and following their own choice. That would certainly release a good deal of staff time for much more personal interactive teaching, but even so I doubt if it would be enough to satisfy the students' needs, without wrecking the other four legs of the five which the university needs to keep healthy.

# Notes

*Figures refer to page numbers*

8 The Human Community project of the Athens Center is described in (July & August 1970 & July 1971) *Ekistics*.

10 The number of the *Futurist* magazine for October 1970 was devoted to the question, 'Is Megalopolis Inevitable?'. There did not seem to be many new ideas for avoiding it, except the conventional 'new towns' approach which has been inadequate up till now.

13 Attempts to use low temperature heat for biological purposes are being made in experiments to exploit warm sea water from nuclear reactors to improve fish farming, or to use warm fresh water for irrigating crops.

15 Platt has elaborated on the idea of the emergency character of the present situation, in an article, 'What we must do' in *Science* **66** (1969) 1115—21.

15 Route 128 is a ring road round Boston, near the Harvard-MIT complex, on which many small firms depending on very sophisticated technology established themselves.

16 There is a good article on this, 'Enzymes: a new technology', by Malcolm D. Lilley & Peter Dunnill, *Science Journal* (April 1969). For a more technical account, *see* I. Silman & E. Katchalski, *Ann Rev. Biochem.*, **35** (1966) 873.

21 See *Single-Cell Protein* p. 297 ed. R. I. Matelas & S. R. Tannenbaum (MIT Press 1968) This book provides references for many of the topics discussed in the last few pages. For a more popular account *see* N. W. Pirie, *Food Resources, Conventional and Novel.* (Penguin Books 1969).

21 *See* Borgstrom, *Centennial Review* (Michigan State University), **2**, 287—311.

23 *See*, for instance, his article in the Nobel Symposium No. 14, 1970, *The Place of Value in a World of Facts.*

24 For a popular article on these techniques, *see* B. Ephrussi & Mary C. Weiss, 'Hybrid somatic cells', *Scientific American.* (April 1969).

25 There is a very general survey in a report of a meeting on Pest Control, in *Science,* **164** (1969) 203.

25 A second symposium organized by IUBS at Seattle, Washington, in May 1971 was centred on this theme. Its proceedings will be published by the University of Washington Press during 1972 under the title *Biology Relevant to Human Welfare.*

30 A chreod is a system containing many components which

interact with one another so that the state of the system changes as time passes; and the interactions are such that they control each other so that the pathway of change is to some extent 'buffered' or 'canalized' — if the system is pushed away from its normal path of change, it will tend to move back on to the normal path at a later time. *See* C. H. Waddington, *The Strategy of the Genes* (Allen & Unwin, 1957) or *Towards a Theoretical Biology, Vol. 1.* ed. C. H. Waddington, (Edinburgh University Press 1968).

37 Robert Rauschenberg, American painter, of the movement that succeeded the New York Abstract Expressionists.

37 Charles Ives, American composer.

38 Marcel Duchamp, French painter, one of the father figures of the Dada movement.

39 *See* Mandelbrot, New methods in statistical economics, *Journal of Political Economy,* **71** (1963) 421.

39 *See* note to p. 30.

39 Alfred Jarry, French author of *Ubu Roi* (1896: English translation Gabberbochus Press, London 1951), an anti-rationalistic Beatnik-lile character. *See* Roger Shattuck, *The Banquet Years* (Harcourt Brace, New York 1955), for an easily accessible account of him.

41 Compare one of the first attempts to fortell the future — H. G. Wells, *The Time Machine,* in which the human race becomes divided into two races, pleasure-loving weaklings and the brutal hard-working Morlocks.

42 *See* note to p. 30.

43 René Thom, French mathematician and topologist. *See* his book *Stabilité Structurelle et Biologie* (Benjamin 1969), or his article in *Towards a Theoretical Biology, Vol. 3,* ed. C. H. Waddington (Edinburgh University Press 1970).

43 *See* Anatol Rapoport, *Strategy and Conscience* (Harper & Row 1964) where Platt has described some experiments on non-zero-sum games in his article.

43 Arp, Hans or Jean, German-French painter-sculptor, one of the first group of Dadaists, *On My Way* (Wittenborn, New York 1968). There is a further discussion of his idea about the 'mindless' order of nature in C. H. Waddington's *Behind Appearance* (Edinburgh and MIT University Presses 1970).

44 *See* E. Schroedinger (one of the founders of quantum physics) *What is Life?* (Cambridge University Press 1944).

44 e.e. cummings (he insists on the lower case initials), American thirties poet. This is from his first book, *Tulips and Chimneys* (Seltzer, New York, 1924).

44 D. T. Suzuki was an influential teacher of Zen in America. There is a paperback of his essays on Zen Buddhism (Doubleday Anchor Books 1956).

46 Marshall McLuhan, Canadian philosopher. His most famous books are *The Gutenberg Galaxy* (Toronto University Press 1962), *Understanding Media* (McGraw-Hill 1964), and *The*

*Medium is the Message* (Banton Books & Random House 1967). For a knock-about argy-bargy see *McLuhan Hot and Cool* (Penguin 1968, and Dial Press, USA 1967).

46 George H. Mead, social psychologist at Chicago: *see* for instance, *Mind, Self and Society from the Standpoint of a Social Behaviourist* (Chicago University Press 1934).

46 *I-Ching* or *Book of Changes,* classical Chinese book for divination by stochastic processes — throwing coins or drawing straws. Best known English translation is from the German of Richard Wilhelm, translated into English by Cary F Baynes with foreword by C. C. Jung (Bollingen Foundation, New York, & Routledge, London).

I quote without comment, a paragraph from a letter to me from Gunther Stent:

'Since John Cage had pointed out to me the analogy between the genetic code and the *I-Ching,* I have looked into this matter a little more. To my amazement I found that the 'natural' order of the *I-Ching* hexagrams generates a table of nucleotide triplet codons which shows the same inter-codon generic relations as Crick's table!'

51 W. H. Auden, poet, English at this time, later American. From *Another Time* (Faber & Faber 1940).

52 *See* H. D. Lasswell in the Nobel Symposium; *see* note to p. 23.

55 Published in *Anarchy,* **88** (1967).

# Index

Abdus Salam, 23
affluent society, 33
Alfred Jarry's Dada Science, 39
alienation, 32
anarchy, 30, 51
animal behaviour, 43
anti-intellectualism, 51
aperiodic crystal, 44
Arp, 43
atomic energy, 13
attractants, 12
Auden, 51
automation, 1

Bach, 29
Beatles, 37
biology and human rights, 58
bioengineering, 22, 23
Biological Bill of Rights, 60
biological control, 15
biological warfare, 15
birth control steroids, 17
*Bulletin of Atomic Scientists*, 64

Calder, Nigel, v
carbon dioxide, 20
cell wall, 18
Caplow, 56
chessboard, 40
*Chlorella*, 20
chreod, 10, 30, 39, 42, 43, 58
communication, 48, 53
community, 9
comprehensive design science, 52
'copping out', 32
culture, 48
cummings, e.e., 44
curriculum, 57
cybernetics, 55

Debussy, 29
decay of motivation, 5
Delbruck, 3
Democritean view, 52
Denmark, 21
desalination, 13
developing countries, 14–17, 19, 21, 34, 49
developing world, 1
disorganization, 30
drone, 24
Duchamp, 36
dwarf wheat, 7

eco-system, 45
Ecumenopolis, 11
education, 51
ekistics, 52
*Environment*, 64
*Ethical Animal, The*, 50
evolution, 3
evolutionary potential, 47
exponential increase, 49

Faustian man, 36
fermentors, 16
fermentation, 14
food, 7
frog, 37
frustration, 32
Fuller, Buckminster, 5, 35, 52
fundamental, 24

Gabor, 40
gap between rich and poor countries, 7
Ghandi, 35
generalist, 52
generation gap, 45
genetics, 38
geography, 38
goals for colleges of education, 62

Golden Age, The, 41
governmental unit, 9
Gregory, R. L., 4
group survival, 31

harmony, 29, 54
heat pollution, 19
Heraclidan view, 52
higher-order system 42
home, 12
human ecology, 55, 63, 64
human settlements, 64
Hutchins, 42
Hutterites, 47
hydrogen, 19
Hydrogenomonas, 19

I Ching, 46
identification, 31
Ideology and Organization, 5
immediate goals, 31
income, 7
inequalities of wealth, 32
insecticide, 12
intellectual urgencies, 5
internal organization, 11
International Rice
  Organization, 8
Ives, Charles, 37, 54

Japanese language, 42
Johns, Jasper, 58

Karl, Henry, 29
Kelly, Elsworth, 58
kibbutz, 47
King, Phillip, 58
de Kooning, 58

language, 57
Lichtenstein, 58
lock-ins, 27
longshoremen, 36

McHale, John, 52
McLuhan, 46
madness, 44
Maori, 41
management structures, 10
Mandelbrot, 39, 40
Manus (tribe), 41

Marcuse, 33
maser, 23
Marx, Karl, 39
maximize, 3, 4, 31
Mead, George, 46
meat analogues, 14, 17-19
megalopolis, 8, 11
Meier, Richard, 9
meson, 23
methane, 19
  fermentation, 22
microbial protein, 17
mindlessness, 37
mitochondrion, 42
model, 27, 28
models of the world, 5
motivation, 47
move into the cities, 10
Mozart, 29
Myth of Sisyphus, 47

neighbourhoods, 8
new product, 17
nitrogen fertilizer, 14
nitrogen fixation, 14, 15, 18
Nobel prize, 22, 23

open-ness, 29
operational research, 43
optimization, 3, 4
organization, 12, 30
origin of language, 29

Paolozzi, 58
participation, 38
participatory democracy, 12
paralyzing society, 34
paraphysics, 34
Pasteur, 23
perception, 4
pheromones, 25
photosynthesis, 15, 20
Piaget, 4
plant breeding, 24
Pollock, Jackson, 58
pollutants, 12
Polynesian, 37
population, 7
  control, 24
  increase, 15, 34

power, 35
prehension, 38
'Prisoners' Dilemma', 43
proteins, 16
psychological needs, 18

Quaker meeting, 37

Rabi, 22
Rattray, Taylor, v
Rauschenberg, 37, 58
*Rhizobia*, 14
Riley, Bridget, 58
Rockefeller Foundation, 13
Rothko, 58
*Route 128*, 15–17
rules of order, 30

*Scenedesmus*, 20
Schlegel, 19
self-stabilizing system, 42
settlement crisis, 8
sewage, 19, 20
   converter, 14
simulation, 27
single-cell protein, 16
solid-phase enzyme, 14
solid-state enzymology, 16
*Spain*, 51
*Spirulina platensis*, 20
starter pill, 14, 18
sterile male, 12
*Step to Man, The*, 38
subject and object, 4
sugar, 16, 17
   cane cells, 16
Suzuki, 44

Syntek company, 16
systems, 42

thermal pollution, 13
'thing' notion, 43
Thoreau, 5, 44
three wishes, 13
transaction, 50
transmission of commitment,
   33

'University is a Five-Legged
   Animal', 53
University of Chicago, 56
urbanization, 2

value systems, 5
Varese, 54
Vassarely, 58
vegetable, 45
veterinary vaccine, 15

Walden Two, 47
WARF, 17
Warhol, 58
waste heat, 13
waste products, 13
welfare, 60
Whitehead, 38
whole undivided entity, 28
World Game, 36
World University, 52

yeast, 17

Zen, 44